Disciples Then!
Disciples Now!
Learning To Follow Jesus

Phyllis Vos Wezeman

Judith Harris Chase

DEDICATION:

To Clarence B. "Whitey" Vos and Dorothy Vos Sikkema, Marion A. and Una Vos, and Harold B. and Jean Vos ... Uncles and Aunts who have modeled discipleship for me. (P.V.W.)

In memory of Leo and Helen Swartz and in honor of Bill and Mabel Wills, youth leaders, who gave generously of their time and talents to nurture young disciples.
(J.H.C.)

DISCIPLES THEN! DISCIPLES NOW!

by Judith Harris Chase and Phyllis Vos Wezeman

Copyright © 1995 Educational Ministries, Inc.

Printed in the United States of America. All rights reserved. No portion of this book may be reproduced by any means without prior permission of the copyright owner.

ISBN: 1-877871-88-5

EDUCATIONAL MINISTRIES, INC.
165 Plaza Drive
Prescott, AZ 86303
800-221-0910

Table Of Contents

OVERVIEW	5
CHAPTER ONE — GALILEE GAZETTE	7
CHAPTER TWO — SIMON PETER	17
CHAPTER THREE — ANDREW	23
CHAPTER FOUR — JAMES	29
CHAPTER FIVE — JOHN	35
CHAPTER SIX — PHILIP	43
CHAPTER SEVEN — BARTHOLOMEW	49
CHAPTER EIGHT — THOMAS	55
CHAPTER NINE — MATTHEW	61
CHAPTER TEN — JAMES THE LESS	69
CHAPTER ELEVEN — JUDE/THADDAEUS	75
CHAPTER TWELVE — SIMON THE ZEALOT	81
CHAPTER THIRTEEN — JUDAS ISCARIOT	87
CHAPTER FOURTEEN — MATTHIAS	93
CHAPTER FIFTEEN — CONCLUSION	99

CHAPTER SIXTEEN — ADAPTATIONS 109

EDUCATOR'S MEDITATION 112

RESOURCES 114

Overview

DISCIPLE

Many terms can be used to define the word "disciple": adherent, apostle, believer, convert, devotee, follower, learner, listener, pupil, student, witness. Basically, a disciple is a pupil or follower of a teacher or school. In this resource, however, the word "disciple" refers to an early follower of Jesus, especially any of the original twelve and one replacement often called the Apostles, and to a follower of Jesus — past, present and future — known by the term "Christian." The exercises and experiences in this book are designed to help participants discover more about the "Disciples Then," and to realize that they are the "Disciples Now."

DISCIPLES THEN!

This book provides information for lessons based on the lives of Jesus' first disciples: Simon Peter, Andrew, James, John, Philip, Bartholomew, Matthew, Thomas, James the Less, Jude/Thaddaeus, Simon the Zealot, Judas Iscariot and Matthias, the replacement for Judas Iscariot. Each chapter explores the mission and ministry of a different follower. Although each chapter contains background information on the disciple, including data on the person's relationship with Jesus and an activity incorporating the individual's traditional symbol, the material for each unit is also organized around a unique theme:

Chapter One — Introduction: <u>Galilee Gazette</u> Newspaper
Chapter Two — Simon Peter: Numbers
Chapter Three — Andrew: Places
Chapter Four — James: Names
Chapter Five — John: The Word
Chapter Six — Philip: Questions
Chapter Seven — Bartholomew: Known by Others
Chapter Eight — Thomas: Twos
Chapter Nine — Matthew: Occupations, Change
Chapter Ten — James the Less: Mystery, Clues
Chapter Eleven — Jude/Thaddaeus: Insights
Chapter Twelve — Simon the Zealot: Qualities of a Disciple
Chapter Thirteen — Judas Iscariot: Contrasts
Chapter Fourteen — Matthias: Rocks

Chapter Fifteen — Conclusion: Twelve
Information for these sessions is taken from scriptural and historical perspectives.

DISCIPLES NOW!

Disciple is a word that refers to a person who followed Jesus long ago, as well as to an individual who follows Jesus today. Using biblical, historical and modern-day examples, learning activities are designed to help participants realize that they are the "Disciples Now."

LEARNING TO FOLLOW JESUS

In <u>Disciples Then! Disciples Now!</u> instruction takes place through involvement in a series of learning centers based on the theme "Following Jesus." Participants explore and experience inviting, informing and inspiring activities that are used to impart information and ideas.

A learning center may be defined as the focal point of activity for the purpose of acquiring knowledge or skill. It must contain information on a topic and instructions for a task. A learning center needs to include the supplies and equipment necessary to complete an assignment or activity. Learning centers may be created in many ways. They may be constructed on tabletops, desks, counters, bulletin boards, chalk boards, walls or any other surface that will hold the essential elements. Learning centers may be extremely efficient, containing the bare essentials required for achieving the desired results, or extraordinarily elaborate with bountiful enhancements to supplement the anticipated outcomes.

Learning centers are used to: create an opportunity for the learning to occur; develop discovery learning techniques; emphasize hands-on experiences; focus attention on specific topics and tasks; foster cooperative learning; promote critical thinking skills; provide self-directed, individualized instruction.

Learning Centers may be used in virtually any educational setting. They are ideal for church school classes, worship centers, children's church, Vacation Bible School, mid-week ministries, kids' clubs, intergenerational events, before and after school care programs, youth groups, retreats, confirmation classes and more. Suggestions for adapting learning centers to other program designs are provided in Chapter Sixteen. Learning centers are for people of all ages — children, youth and adults. Designed especially for individual students, learning centers also work well for small group projects.

Provided in an easy-to-use format, the activities for each chapter list the materials required for the project, offer directions for advance preparation and give complete directions for accomplishing the task. If the activity is to be used in a learning center, the instructions must be copied and placed in the display together with the required supplies. <u>Disciples Then! Disciples Now! Learning To Follow Jesus</u> is a valuable resource for anyone involved in the worship, education, outreach and nurture ministries of a congregation. It is also appropriate for use in school and home. May all who use this volume rejoice in the legacy left by the early followers of Jesus and respond to the lessons learned by those who follow Jesus today.

Chapter One

Galilee Gazette

Extra! Extra! Read all about it! "Jesus Chooses Twelve Disciples!" Although this news made the headlines thousands of years ago, the significance of this story is as important now as it was then. Jesus' call to his first special group of followers not only changed their lives and the lives of their families and friends, it changed our lives as well. Because the selection of the twelve disciples was such an important consideration, Jesus spent the entire night praying to his Father before he came to his decision (Luke 6:12-13). These twelve people would be chosen, called, taught and commissioned to be the Messianic community, first to the "lost sheep of the house of Israel," and then to the world at large. They would be the ones responsible for carrying on Jesus' ministry after he was no longer on earth. Though the commission to go into all the world to preach the Gospel and to baptize believers (Matthew 28:18-20) was entrusted to the twelve men Jesus called during Bible times, it has been passed on through the ages and is ours today. Since Jesus has chosen each of us who are his followers as his modern day disciples, we can learn much from the first disciples of Jesus, using them as our example for the work we are to do in today's world. This headline news of thousands of years ago continues as an important story today.

Eight experiences in this learning center focus on the call of the first disciples and explore themes such as the meaning of discipleship, the significance of the number twelve and the settings in which Jesus taught his followers. Using the format of a newspaper, each participant will have the opportunity to create and complete projects at each center for his or her own edition of The Galilee Gazette. As the learning center activities are introduced, provide each pupil with a large sheet of paper such as newsprint, 12" x 18" construction paper or 11" x 17" copy paper. Each learning center will contain information and supplies for various sections of the paper. After pictures are drawn, stories are written or activities are completed, the "lay out" should be arranged in an attractive format and attached to the newspaper sheet.

Besides gathering the basic supplies for the eight centers, advance preparation will be required to duplicate the word search game, reproduce the map, assemble the Passover foods and record the "Disciples" song onto a cassette tape.

LEAD STORY --- JESUS CHOOSES TWELVE DISCIPLES

Supplies:
- ❑ Paper
- ❑ Bibles
- ❑ Tape player
- ❑ Pens
- ❑ Cassette tape of "Disciples" song
- ❑ Glue

Advance Preparation:

- Record "Disciples" song onto a cassette tape. Go through hymnals and songbooks you have and find a favorite song on the Disciples. Some suggestions are: "There Were Twelve Disciples" by George Minor and "Twelve Is Not Enough" by Ted Wuerffel, <u>Sing A Song Of Scripture</u>, Lillenas Publishing Co., 1986; "There Were Twelve" by Anne Rupp, <u>Sing and Be Glad: Foundation Series Songs From Grades 1-8</u>, Evangel Press, Faith & Life Press, Mennonite Publishing House, 1986; "The Twelve Disciples" by Helen Friesen, <u>Celebrate Jesus</u>, Shining Star Publications, 1988; "The Twelve Disciples" by Wilson Lee Augsburger, <u>Action, Vol. 2,</u> Zondervan Publishing House, 1947.

Compose the lead story for the <u>Galilee Gazette</u>: "Jesus Chooses Twelve Disciples." Following the technique of a good reporter, be sure the article includes answers to the five W's of journalism: Who, What, When, Where and Why. Develop the news report around questions such as: Who were the twelve disciples Jesus chose? What is a disciple? When were these men selected? Where did they receive their training? Why did Jesus need disciples?

Find the answers to these questions by listening to a tape-recorded version of traditional or contemporary music about the twelve disciples. The names of the twelve are contained in the words of the song. Play the song and write down the answers to the five "W" questions. Listen to the cassette tape several times to obtain enough information for the story. Refer to Luke 6:12-16 in the New Testament for additional information and for the correct spelling of the disciples' names. Write a news story containing factual information about the call of the twelve disciples. Arrange the "copy" in columns on the front page of the <u>Galilee Gazette</u>.

Discovery Page---
Significance Of The Number Twelve

Supplies:
- ❑ 12 Tribes Word Search Game
- ❑ Bibles
- ❑ Paper
- ❑ Pencils
- ❑ Glue
- ❑ Duplicating equipment

Advance Preparation:
- Duplicate Word Search Game.

Jesus called twelve disciples to learn from him and to continue his ministry in the world. It is not surprising that Jesus chose twelve people, since that number is significant for many reasons. Historically, the number twelve symbolizes the closeness of God with man.[1] Twelve is mentioned repeatedly in the scriptures, for example, 12 years, 12 wells in Elim, 12 silver bowls, 12 golden spoons and 12 bullocks. In addition, there are many multiples of twelve listed in the Bible. Most importantly, there were 12 tribes of Israel. Jesus intentionally selected twelve special disciples to represent the New Israel and to guarantee the continuation of God's mercy and blessing to all nations of the earth.

Try to identify the twelve tribes of Israel. Remember that they are named for the twelve sons of Jacob. Look up Genesis 35:23-26 for clues. Discover the names of the twelve in this passage and use a pencil to circle them in the word search game. They may be arranged horizontally, vertically or diagonally. Attach the word search to a section of the newspaper.

Find the following names in the word search.

- ❑ ISSACHAR
- ❑ BENJAMIN
- ❑ JOSEPH
- ❑ SIMEON
- ❑ ASHER
- ❑ DAN

- ❑ NAPHTALI
- ❑ ZEBULUN
- ❑ REUBEN
- ❑ JUDAH
- ❑ LEVI
- ❑ GAD

```
N  A  S  H  E  R  X  H  R  O  D  X
N  A  C  X  N  K  P  J  U  D  A  H
A  A  P  B  K  E  R  E  U  B  E  N
X  G  D  H  S  L  E  O  I  C  I  O
L  E  A  O  T  Z  E  B  U  L  U  N
X  Z  J  Q  G  A  S  V  N  S  L  L
Z  S  T  Q  A  R  L  I  D  S  M  J
L  E  V  I  D  S  M  I  M  E  Y  T
H  R  Q  A  V  Q  D  M  Z  E  P  C
S  R  A  H  C  A  S  S  I  U  O  G
C  V  B  E  N  J  A  M  I  N  Q  N
V  B  K  A  L  L  O  H  I  L  U  E
```

Disciples Then! Disciples Now! — 9

EDITORIAL PAGE----FOLLOWING JESUS

Supplies:
- Paper
- Glue
- Pencils

The Twelve disciples were called to travel with Jesus for on-the-job training. They were required to leave behind their jobs, families, possessions and comforts. Jesus warned that being his followers would not be easy. If Jesus came to you today and said, "Follow Me!" would you go? Would you be willing to leave everything and follow him? It might be more difficult to leave some things than others. Make one list of things that would be easy to leave behind and another list of things that would be difficult to leave behind.

Fold a paper in half vertically and write these phrases across the top:

<u>EASY TO LEAVE</u>   <u>DIFFICULT TO LEAVE</u>

List as many ideas as possible under each heading.

Interview other people about this topic. Talk with classmates, teachers, parents and members of the congregation. Write their answers under the two headings. Compare the answers of older and younger "risk-takers." Use the lists to write a "Letter to the Editor." State the issue, such as following or risk-taking. Explain the purpose of the letter. Give opinions on the topic, supported by two or three reasons. Make a strong closing argument to convince people to agree or to take specific actions. Add the letter to a page of the newspaper.

CLASSIFIED ADS----JOB DESCRIPTION OF A DISCIPLE

Supplies:
- Bibles
- Pens
- Paper
- Glue

In Matthew 10:1, 5-14, Jesus provides a job description of a disciple. Look up this passage in the Bible and read it carefully. Make a list of all the things the disciples were to do. Use this information to write a classified ad for the position of a disciple. For example:

> **DISCIPLES WANTED.** *Twelve men needed to follow Jewish Rabbi. Must be able to cast out demons, cure diseases and seek the lost. Come as you are, leave everything behind. On-the-job training. Travel rations. No pay.*

Write a Classified Ad for the job of "Disciple" and add it to the last page of the newspaper.

Pictorial Essay----How The Disciples Learned From Jesus

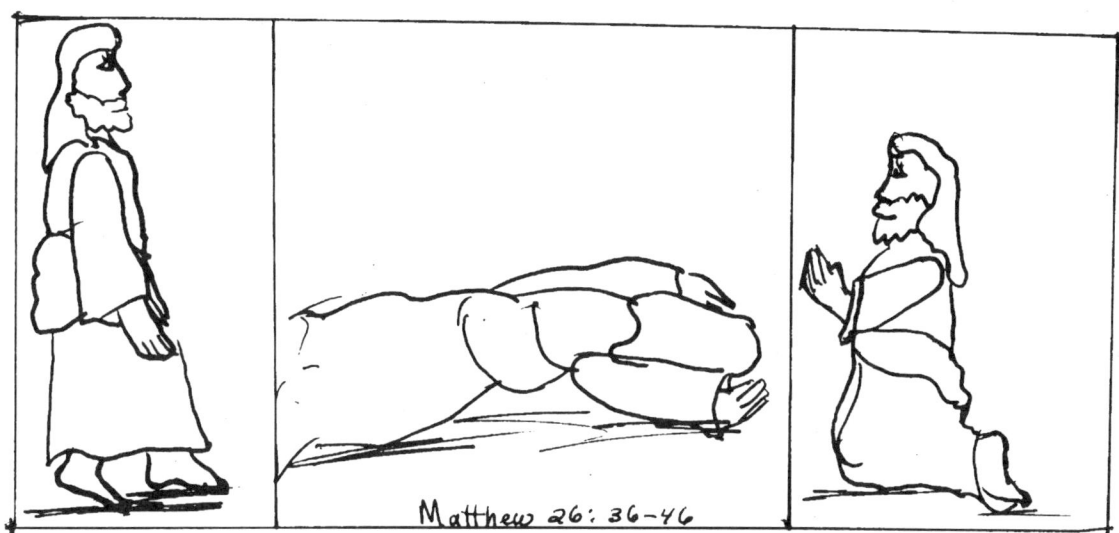

Supplies:
- ❏ White paper
- ❏ Pencils
- ❏ Glue
- ❏ Markers
- ❏ Bibles

Jesus prayerfully selected twelve men to be his personal disciples (Luke 6:12-13). As Jesus' pupils, these important followers were constantly with their teacher, watching and listening as he taught, healed, argued, blessed and prayed. Jesus shared every part of his life with the twelve in order to prepare them to continue his ministry.

The disciples learned from their teacher by observing him in many different situations. Look in the Bible to discover some of the events the disciples witnessed. Suggested scripture passages to use include: Matthew 8:1-4—Jesus Cleanses a Leper; Matthew 8:23-27—Jesus Stills the Storm; Matthew 21:1-11—Jesus' Triumphal Entry; Matthew 21:12-13—Jesus Cleanses the Temple; and Matthew 26:36-46—Jesus Prays in Gethsemane. Divide a piece of paper into three sections. Choose one event for the picture essay and illustrate it in the three frames. Or, draw one frame to portray the way Jesus taught the disciples to pray, another to depict Jesus' miracles and a third to show Jesus teaching the crowds.

As you read about the ways in which Jesus taught the disciples, you will personally learn more about Jesus' teachings, too. Lay out the pictorial essay on a page of the newspaper and glue it in place.

TRAVEL PAGE—MAP OF AREA OF JESUS' MINISTRY

Supplies:
- Bible
- Map
- Glue
- Duplicating equipment.
- Bible atlas
- Colored pencils and pens
- Paper

Advance Preparation:
- Duplicate map on following page

The twelve disciples observed Jesus performing miracles that showed his power and proved he was the Son of God. Jesus demonstrated power over nature, sickness, evil spirits and death. Use the references given for Trips A, B, C or D and learn about the area around the Sea of Galilee. With a Bible and a Bible atlas, plan your own "Miles of Miracles" Tour!

Trip A — Power Over Nature
- John 2:1-11—*Turns water to wine*
- Matthew 14:22-23—*Walks on sea*
- Matthew 21:17-22—*Withers fig tree*

Trip B — Power Over Sickness
- Mark 2:1-12—*Heals paralyzed man*
- Matthew 12:9-14—*Heals crippled hand*
- Matthew 15:21-28—*Heals non-Jewish girl*

Trip C — Power Over Evil Spirits
- Mark 1:23-27—*Sends evil spirits from man*
- Luke 11:14—*Heals man who couldn't talk*

Trip D — Power Over Death
- Matthew 9:18-26—*Raises Jairus' daughter*
- Luke 7:11-16—*Raises widow's only son*

Choose the miracle tour of your preference and mark the location of each event on a copy of the map. Refer to an atlas to see if you will be in the mountains or on the water. Have a safe trip, and add the page to the "Travel Section" of the newspaper.

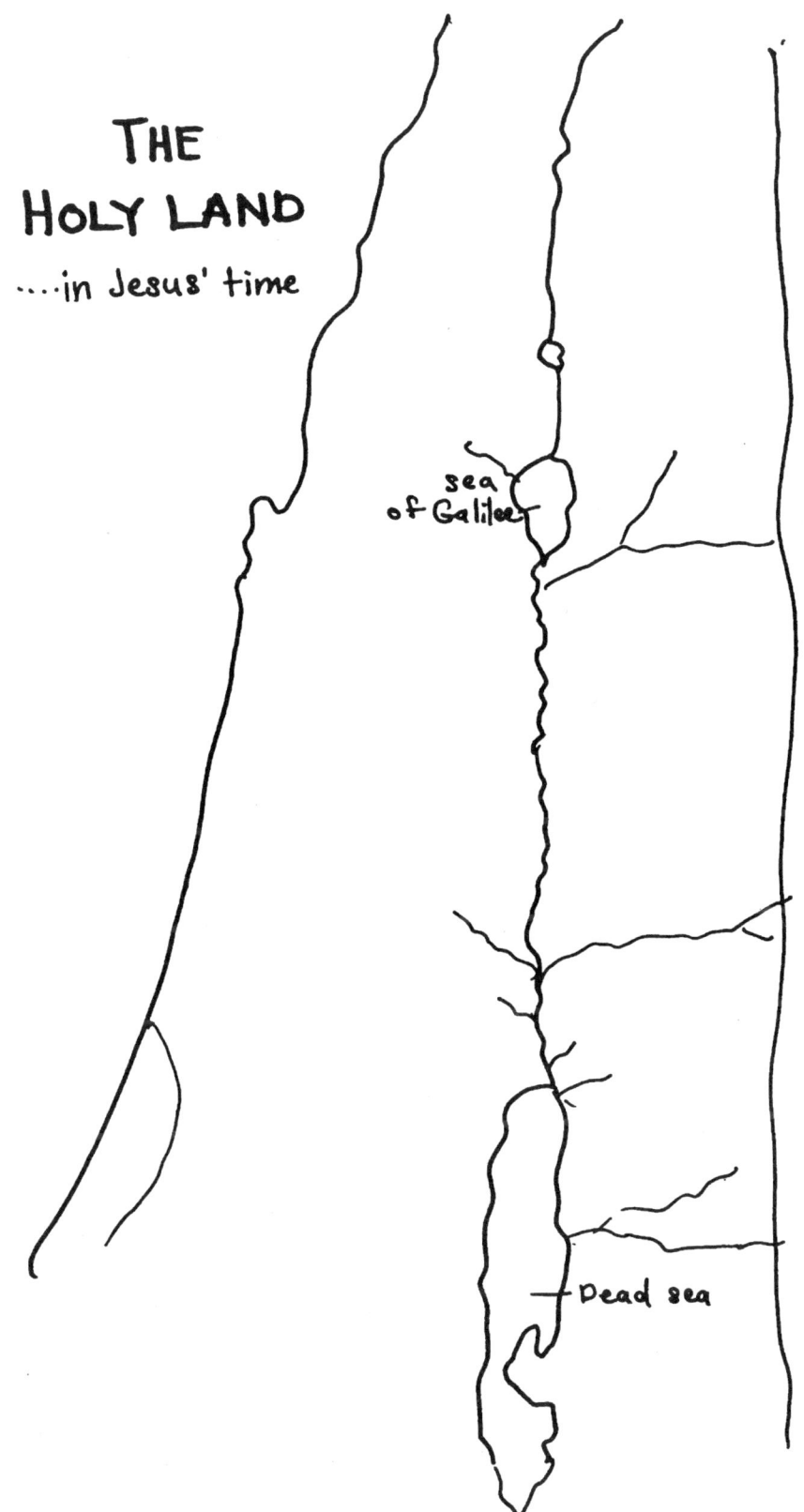

FOOD SECTION ---SYMBOLIC FOODS OF JESUS' TIME

Supplies:
- ❑ Lamb bone
- ❑ Parsley
- ❑ Nuts
- ❑ Wine or grape juice
- ❑ Paper
- ❑ Glue
- ❑ Unleavened bread
- ❑ Chopped apples
- ❑ Cinnamon
- ❑ Plates
- ❑ Markers

Prepare a special edition of the "Food Section" of the newspaper, featuring the symbolic elements of the Passover meal.

Passover, a solemn sacrificial meal, commemorates the Israelites' deliverance from the Pharaoh of Egypt. Jesus, as well as the disciples, would have observed Passover many times throughout their lives. Jesus celebrated the Passover with his disciples in the Upper Room on the day of Holy Week, referred to as Maundy Thursday.

Unscramble the words to identify each symbolic item in the display. Read the descriptions for clues. Once each item is identified, draw a picture and write a brief description of it for the feature story. Attach the food section to a page of the <u>Galilee Gazette</u>.

CLUES

SSAEORH

A mixture of chopped apples, nuts, cinnamon and wine, with its reddish color it recalls the mortar used by the Jews in building the palaces and pyramids of Egypt during their years of forced labor.

ENWI

Four cups are drunk during the course of the Passover meal, because the book of Exodus records four different words, all signifying redemption, spoken by God when He sent Moses to deliver the Jews.

ZASTOM

Called the bread of affliction, it was made of flour

and water only. It represented the bread baked by the Jews during their hasty flight from Egypt, when there was not time for leavening to allow the bread to rise.

TTRRBBEEIHS

Dipped in vinegar or salt, this reminded the people of the difficulty of their slavery and suffering in Egypt.

MBLA

Representative of the animal which was sacrificed in the temple, it served to remind the Jews of the blood that saved their ancestors at the time of the exodus.

ENTERTAINMENT PAGE---JESUS FOLLOWS PRECEDENT IN CHOOSING DISCIPLES

Supplies:
- ❑ Bibles
- ❑ Paper
- ❑ Glue
- ❑ Reference books
- ❑ Colored pencils

When Jesus gathered a group of disciples to learn from him and to carry out his mission, he was following a precedent set in Old Testament and New Testament times. In Isaiah 8:16 the prophet declares, "Bind up the testimony and seal up the law among my disciples." Isaiah's disciples were the ones who gathered, preserved and protected the sermons, oracles, poems and hymns of the prophet.

Judaism preserved and interpreted the Old Testament through the institution of the rabbi and his disciples. Although God was the primary teacher of the Law, the rabbi was both the reader and interpreter of God's will for each individual Israelite. Students who aspired to become rabbis served an apprenticeship or became disciples with a rabbi of their choice. Once they became rabbis, their own disciples, or learners, gathered around them.

When John the Baptist appeared out of the Judean wilderness to herald the coming of the Messiah and to proclaim the baptism of repentance for the forgiveness of sins, crowds gathered around him, forming a company of disciples. Among John's companions there was a group from Galilee, which included his cousin, Jesus of Nazareth. In fact, Jesus was baptized by John, and during this event there was a special revelation by God that Jesus was the Messiah. The Gospel of John suggests that Jesus' first followers dated from this event, when they began, at John the Baptist's encouragement, to follow Jesus instead of John.

Jesus had many followers, or disciples; however, he chose twelve special people who were to be an integral part of his ministry. To these twelve disciples Jesus invested himself and entrusted his teachings. They were the ones who could testify to what God had done in sending His special Son.

Using the information on the historical significance of disciples, design an advertisement for an epic movie about disciples throughout history, or a series of documentaries about disciples of Isaiah, the rabbis, John the Baptist and Jesus. The ad should include a title for the story, highlights of the film and the names of the actors and actresses. Also write a review of the film that will interest people in going to see it. Draw pictures to illustrate the theme. Add the page to the entertainment section of the newspaper.

ANSWERS

Twelve Tribes Word Search:

WORD	ROW	COL	DIR
ISSACHAR	10	9	W
NAPHTALI	1	1	SE
BENJAMIN	11	3	E
ZEBULUN	5	6	E
JOSEPH	6	3	NE
REUBEN	3	7	E
SIMEON	6	7	SE
JUDAH	2	8	E
ASHER	1	2	E
LEVI	8	1	E
DAN	4	3	NW
GAD	6	5	S

Food Section:

Haroses; Wine; Matzos; Bitter Herbs; Lamb.

[1] Davis, Michael. *Young Reader's Book of Christian Symbols*. Nashville: Abingdon, 1967.

Chapter Two

Simon Peter

One. Two. Three. Fifty. Three thousand. Many numbers come to mind when one thinks about the life of Simon Peter. As number one, he was the first disciple to be called to follow Jesus. Although little is known about his life before this time, the Bible states that Simon and his brother Andrew, sons of John, were fishermen with him on the Sea Of Galilee. In fact, they were partners with the sons of Zebedee, James and John, who were also called to be disciples. Simon was instructed to leave his nets and fish for people. During the course of his ministry, Jesus gave Simon a second name, Peter, for a very special reason. Peter's words, recorded in Matthew 16:16, Mark 8:29 and Luke 9:20, form the basis for the creeds and confessions of the church today. Three times Peter denied Jesus, and three times Peter was assured of Jesus' love and forgiveness. Fifty days after Jesus' Resurrection, on the day of Pentecost, Peter was filled with the Holy Spirit and preached a powerful sermon, resulting in the conversion of at least three thousand new believers. These numbers, and others, form the structure for the activities in the learning centers about Peter. Use the lessons to help the participants learn more about the countless ways in which Peter's ministry and mission influenced the early church and the church today.

ONE

Supplies:

- Cardboard
- Scissors
- Bibles
- Posterboard or manila file folders
- Pens

Advance Preparation:

- Draw a large number one on heavy paper. Cut the shape into eight jigsaw puzzle pieces. On each shape write a scripture reference that describes one of Peter's "firsts." Also write the "first" on the back of the piece.
- Include:
  - Matthew 4:18-20—First disciple called
  - I Corinthians 15:5—First apostle to whom Jesus appeared after the resurrection
  - Acts 2—First leader of the Christian community and the early church following the crucifixion and resurrection

Disciples Then! Disciples Now!

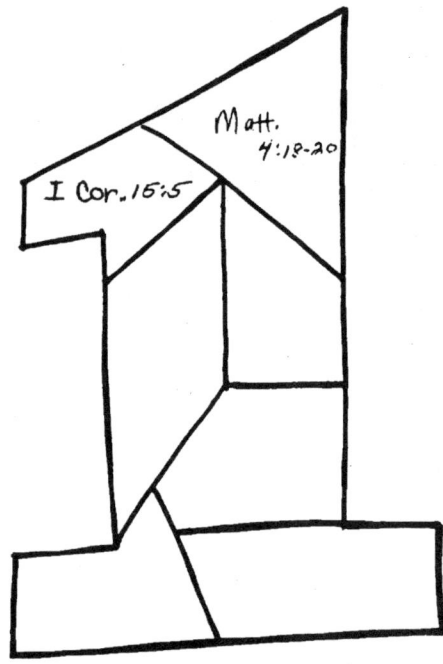

- Acts 10—Admitted the first Gentile, Cornelius, to baptism
- Matthew 16:13-19—First to acknowledge Jesus' divinity
- Matthew 26:35, 69-75—First disciple to deny Jesus
- Acts 5:15—Performed first healing miracle
- Matthew 8:14-17—First to witness Jesus perform miracles

When you think about the life of Simon Peter, what number comes to mind? One! As a disciple of Jesus, Peter was "first" in many ways. Use the puzzle pieces to discover some of the special firsts in Peter's life. Look up the scripture passage written on each puzzle piece, read the verses, and decide on the "first." Check your answer on the back of the piece. Put all the pieces together and see what they form.

TWO

Supplies:
- ❑ Smooth stones
- ❑ Paint brushes
- ❑ Water
- ❑ Name book
- ❑ Acrylic or tempera paint
- ❑ Containers
- ❑ Permanent markers

The first disciple Jesus chose had two names. Originally called Simon, the Greek word for the Hebrew name Symeon, Jesus conferred a new name on his special follower. Jesus gave Simon the Aramaic title of <u>Kepha</u>, which means rock. Using Greek letters to transliterate the word, it comes out Cephas. Translated into Greek, the word is <u>Petros</u>. The Greek equivalent becomes Peter in English. Actually, the designation is more of a descriptive title than a name. Look up Matthew 16:16-19 to see what Jesus told Peter when he gave him the new name. Jesus declared that Peter's confession that Jesus was the Messiah would be the foundation, or rock, of the future church. In some places in the New Testament, Simon Peter is called Simon Bar-Jona, which means Simon, son of John.

Select a rock and use it to serve as a reminder of the special name and its significance that Jesus gave to Simon. Use the paints, brushes and water to write words such as Simon Peter, and to draw symbols on one side of the rock. Allow the colors to dry. Permanent markers may be used to outline, to add details or to print short Bible passages on the stone. Use the name book to look up the meaning of your name. Write your name and its meaning, then draw symbols on

18 — *Disciples Then! Disciples Now!*

the other side of the rock.

Use the painted rock as a reminder of the special ministry Peter had, and you have too, to spread the message of Jesus' love to many people.

THREE

Supplies:
- Balance or scale
- Pencils or pens
- 3 x 5 cards, two colors
- Bible

Advance Preparation:
- Write out several 3 x 5 cards with a mistake or problem on one color card, and the solution or forgiveness on the other color card. Mix each stack of cards. Example:

    Problem—You take a cupcake out of a classmate's lunch. When the person discovers it missing, you say that you didn't do it.

    Solution—You admit that you did wrong, and replace the cupcake.

    Write instructions for playing the game and for using the scale.

Peter and his brother Andrew were the first disciples to be chosen. In the beginning, Peter often had a difficult time being a follower of Jesus. He kept doing and saying many of the wrong things. Jesus said that Peter would deny him three times. Deny means to say something is not the truth or to ignore the truth. Read Mark 14:53-54 and Mark 14:66-72 to learn about Peter's denial of Jesus. Peter felt badly that he made wrong choices. The good news is that even though Peter denied Jesus three times, Jesus forgave Peter three times. Read this important story in John 21:4-17.

Just as Jesus forgives sins, Christians are supposed to forgive others when they do something wrong. Play this matching game to discover some of the ways forgiveness can balance mistakes.

Look through the problem cards and the solution cards. Select a mistake card and match it with a response card. If you have a scale, put the problem cards on one side and the forgiveness cards on the other. Your scale will be out of balance unless there are an equal number of cards on each side. If you don't have a scale, just match the cards with the proper responses.

Write a card for a time that you did something wrong and one for how the mistake was forgiven. Write another card about something wrong that was done to you, and what you did to forgive the person. Add these cards to the match game or scale, or keep them for yourself. Conclude with a silent prayer thanking God for forgiveness through Jesus, the Savior.

Disciples Then! Disciples Now! — 19

SIX

Supplies:
- Bibles
- Markers
- Scissors
- Pictures or patterns of symbols
- Yarn
- Pencils
- 12" x 18" construction paper
- Glue sticks
- Paper scraps
- Hole punch

Advance Preparation:
- Find or develop patterns for Peter's symbols. Provide patterns for the shield and cross, as well.

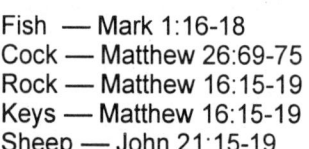

Scripture, legends and traditions influence the apostles' symbols which appear in Christian art. Many of the symbols indicate how the disciple lived or died. Peter is represented by at least six different emblems: fish, cock, keys, rock, sheep and an inverted Latin cross. Writers of early Christian history related that Peter was crucified on an upside-down cross. He did not feel worthy to be executed in the same manner as Jesus. Look up Bible passages and create a shield-shaped banner as a reminder of Peter's life and ministry.

Look up the following scripture references to learn about Peter's life and some of the symbols associated with it:

Fish — Mark 1:16-18
Cock — Matthew 26:69-75
Rock — Matthew 16:15-19
Keys — Matthew 16:15-19
Sheep — John 21:15-19

Trace and cut out the shield shape using construction paper. With a contrasting color, trace and cut out the Latin cross, and attach it to the center of the shield. Design the remaining symbols using markers or paper scraps. Position them around the arms of the cross. Write Peter's name on the banner with a marker.

Punch holes on each side of the shield at the top. Tie yarn through the holes and hang the symbols as a reminder of Peter's life.

FIFTY

Supplies:
- Bibles
- Pens or pencils
- Paper

On the Jewish Festival of Pentecost, fifty days after the resurrection of Jesus, the followers of the ascended Lord were gathered together in Jerusalem when an amazing event took place. Suddenly from heaven there came the sound of a violent wind. Tongues, like fire, rested on each person, and they were filled with the Holy Spirit. Read this story in Acts 2. After reading about the events that took place on this important fiftieth day, re-tell them in a unique way by writing several of the verses as a rebus story. A rebus story consists of pictures that stand for certain words or phrases.

Take a sheet of paper and a pencil or pen and re-write portions of the story in the rebus format. Think of symbols for some of the significant words or phrases, or for words that are repeated often. For example, draw the face of a man to represent Peter, a swaying tree branch to symbolize the wind and a flame for the tongues of fire. Other suggestions would be to draw several people standing together for the crowd and a dove for the Holy Spirit. Begin with verses such as Acts 2:1-4; 32-36; 37-42. Write or paraphrase each line, substituting symbols for some of the words. Remember to use the picture each time the word, such as Peter, is repeated.

Display the rebus story on a bulletin board for others to try to read.

ONE HUNDRED FIFTY

Supplies:
- ❑ Bibles
- ❑ Construction paper
- ❑ Glue
- ❑ Miscellaneous materials
- ❑ Shoe boxes with lids
- ❑ Scissors
- ❑ Tape

Peter is mentioned so often in the New Testament, the Gospels, the Acts and the Epistles of Paul, that there are numerous stories about his life and work once he was called to be a disciple. Depending on the source of information, Peter's name is mentioned in the Bible well over one hundred fifty times. Some reference books say 182 times!

Look up the name Peter in a concordance. A concordance is an alphabetical list of the words in a book, such as the Bible, with references to the passages where they occur. Scan the list to discover all the verses that contain information about the life of Peter. Choose some of the references and look them up in the Bible. Pick one special story and depict it in the form of a "peek box". Follow these simple instructions to make it.

Take the top off of a shoe box and set it aside. Cut a hole in one of the ends of the box. Create a scene inside of the box, facing the hole. Decorate the sides of the box to show where the scene takes place. Tape or glue paper to indicate sky or walls. Cover the bottom of the box to depict the floor or ground. Make figures for people, animals, furniture or whatever is needed. Use paper and other materials to make the figures. Attach the figures to the bottom of the box with tape or glue. The pieces that are most important should be near the front. Cut a slit in the box top to let in the light. Tape the top to the shoe box and decorate the outside of the container. Write the scripture passage that is being illustrated on the outside of the box. Share the story with other people.

Disciples Then! Disciples Now!

COUNTLESS NUMBERS

Supplies:
- ❏ Paper scraps, assorted colors
- ❏ Pencils or pens
- ❏ String
- ❏ Cake pan or low-cut box
- ❏ Fish patterns
- ❏ Large paper clips
- ❏ Magnet
- ❏ Bibles

Advance Preparation:

- Tie the magnet to the string, then attach the string to the dowel to form a fishing pole.
- Trace and cut fish for every class member, plus a few extras. Write a challenge on each fish, such as:
    - Read a story about Jesus to a younger child.
    - Tell someone a story you remember.
    - Invite a friend to Sunday School.
    - Give a toy to someone who needs one.
    - Say kind words to a person who looks sad.
- Fold each fish and paper clip it shut so the words are hidden inside. Place the fish in the low container.

Jesus chose Peter, a fisherman, to become a disciple. Jesus challenged the disciples to be fishers of people, and eventually directed them to go out into the world to share this message. On the day of Pentecost, Peter, the leader of the disciples, preached the sermon, and afterwards many people became Christians. Read Acts 2:37-42 to see the results of Peter's fishing for people. How many people became Christians after his sermon? Later Peter traveled to many places throughout the world to share the message of Jesus' love and countless numbers accepted Jesus as their Savior.

Complete this fishing activity and go out into the world with your own challenge for the week. Use the mini-fishing pole and the magnet to "catch" a fish. Angle the line over the fish until one attaches to the magnet. Unfold the paper and read the "challenge for the week" written inside the fish. Try your very best to do what the challenge suggests. Peter influenced thousands of people, and you can do your part by helping someone learn about Jesus.

Chapter Three

Andrew

Andrew was one of Jesus' first twelve disciples. The name Andrew is Greek, and its original form, Andreas, means "manly." Andrew came from Bethsaida, an area where people spoke Greek and were acquainted with Greek culture. Although Bethsaida was Andrew's initial hometown, his life as a disciple and apostle of Jesus Christ took him to many places. Regardless of the location in which Andrew ministered, his mission was to invite people to know more about the Messiah. Learn about Andrew's life through the theme of locations in which he shared the love of Jesus, by using these learning center activities.

BETHSAIDA

Supplies:
- Paper plates
- Glue
- Markers
- Clear or blue plastic wrap
- Sand
- Paper clips
- Paper punch
- Scissors
- Construction paper
- Stapler
- Cellophane
- Pebbles
- Bible

Andrew was a fisherman. He, together with his brother Simon Peter and his father, operated a small fishing boat on the Sea of Galilee. Most likely, Andrew lived in the same house with Simon Peter (Mark 1:29) in the town of Bethsaida, located on a plain Northeast of where the Jordan River enters the Sea of Galilee. Soon after Andrew met Jesus and acknowledged him to be the Messiah, Jesus invited Andrew to leave his nets and to start fishing for people.

Make an underwater scene which depicts Andrew's original occupation as a fisherman. Begin by cutting the center out of one paper plate, leaving a narrow rim. With the rim of the paper plate right side up, put a line of glue along the inside edge. Stretch clear or blue plastic wrap across the opening and glue it in place to create a window effect. When the glue dries, cut off the excess plastic.

Cut a variety of fish shapes from construction paper and use markers to decorate them. Glue the fish, along with pieces of tissue paper and cellophane, plus sand and pebbles, to the center of a second paper plate. Place the first plate

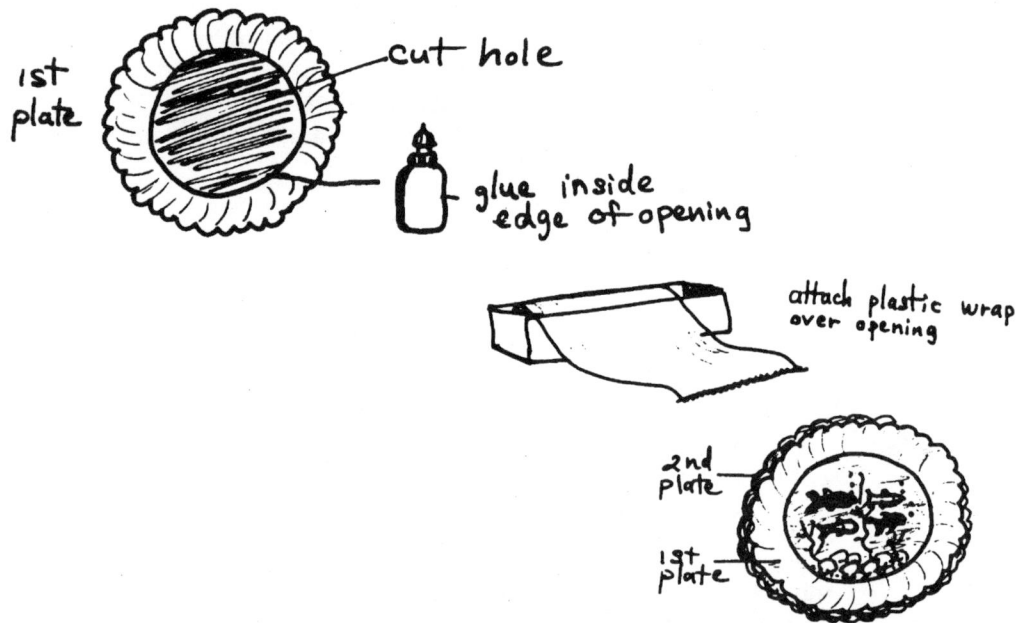

upside down on the second plate and staple the outside edges together. Form a hanger from yarn, string or wire. Punch a hole through the top of the scene and attach the hanger through it.

BETHANY

Supplies:
- Plain stationary or note paper
- Markers
- Pens or pencils
- Bible
- Envelopes
- Stickers
- Stamps

As a disciple of John the Baptist, Andrew saw Jesus' baptism and heard John say, "Behold, the Lamb of God." Later, Jesus invited Andrew to see where he was staying. After spending a day with Jesus, Andrew was convinced that Jesus was the Messiah. He then went to his brother, Simon, and introduced him to Jesus. Read about it in John 1:28-42. The next time the brothers are mentioned, Jesus is extending a special invitation to the two men: "Follow me and I will make you fishers of people." (Matthew 4:19-20)

Today people invite others to their homes to visit and to get better acquainted. Was that why Jesus invited the two men to spend the day with him? Andrew invited his brother to meet his new friend, Jesus. Once Jesus knew Andrew and Peter, Jesus extended a greater invitation: to follow him and in turn to invite others to follow him, too. Make plans to invite someone to visit your home —to play, have lunch, do homework or share a hobby. Ask permission first! Instead of just asking, create an invitation to give to the person.

Design an invitation for a new person in your school or church, for someone you would like to know better, or for a special friend. Fold the paper in half or use the front of already folded paper. Draw or choose stickers that tell something about yourself and what you enjoy, or select emblems representing what you and your invited guest might do together. For example, if you want to ride bikes or listen to music, draw a bike or use music symbol stickers. Inside, write out the day, time and place for the special meeting. You may want to include some ideas for planned activities. Introduce your visitor to family members and friends. Another time, you might invite this person to church or to church school.

SERMON ON THE MOUNT

Supplies:
- Wooden disks, large and small
- Sandpaper
- Wire
- Wire cutters
- Pencils
- Clean-up supplies
- Scissors
- Hand drill with smallest bit
- Paints
- Brushes
- Cord or yarn
- Small fish pattern
- Water
- Bible

Advance Preparation:
- Pre-drill holes. Drill one hole in the top of the large circle and five small holes along the bottom. Drill a tiny hole in the top of each of the small disks. Older classes might be able to drill holes with supervision. Provide an old cutting board or wood plank to place under the disks so drills do not mar table tops.

There is not a lot written about Andrew in the Bible. He appears to have been a quiet, dependable leader, not a "front and center" personality. However, others seemed to rely on him for help. When a crowd of 5,000 followers of Jesus needed to be fed, Andrew was the disciple who found the boy with the five barley loaves and two fish. Sometimes the miracle of "loaves and fishes" is referred to as "five and two." Make a pendant with this symbol as a reminder of this miracle.

Lightly sand the wooden pieces. Trace or draw freehand two simple fish shapes onto the natural wood surface. Paint the fish, adding texture or details. Add the five natural wood "loaves" by threading wire or cord through the holes. Twist the wire or knot the thread, allowing the "loaves" to hang down from the larger circle. Write on the back of the wood: John 6:8-9. Slip a piece of yarn or cord through the hole at the top and adjust it to fit around the neck. Wear the pendant and be able to explain the symbol representing Jesus' miracle and Andrew's part in the event.

JERUSALEM

Supplies:

- ❏ Bible
- ❏ Pens
- ❏ Paper

Andrew will always be remembered as the disciple who brought other people to Jesus. During the week of the Lord's passion, some Greek-speaking worshipers who had come to Jerusalem to celebrate the Passover requested an audience with Jesus. These people approached Philip, a disciple with a Greek name who spoke the Greek language. Not knowing what to do with the request, Philip conferred with the Greek-speaking Andrew. Andrew played the role of intermediary, conveying the message to Jesus (John 12:20-22). Andrew brought the Greeks to Jesus so they could hear of the Good News which was for all people, not just a select group. Remember this important part of Andrew's story by writing a poem about it. Use a five line diamond-shaped format. The formula is as follows:

Line One: One word which is an opposite of line five.
Line Two: Two words which describe line one.
Line Three: Three words which resolve the conflict.
Line Four: Two words which describe line five.
Line Five: One word which is an opposite of line one.

A sample poem might be:

> Seeking
> Greek travelers
> Introduced by Andrew
> Jesus. Messiah.
> Finding

Compose one or more poems about this scripture story and use a pen to record them on paper.

GREECE

Supplies:

- ❏ Pencils
- ❏ Bible
- ❏ Tracing paper
- ❏ Children's Bible atlas or general atlas

In the Greek Orthodox tradition, Andrew is the most beloved of Christ's Apostles. In the time of the early church, Andrew was called <u>protokletos</u>, "the first to be called." He is reported to have preached the Gospel in Asia Minor, in Greece, around Constantinople (Istanbul) and along the coast of the Black Sea. It is recorded that St. Andrew converted thousands of people and founded many parishes throughout those areas. Compared to some of the other disciples,

Andrew was a quiet, but responsible person. He proved his leadership abilities and commitment to Jesus by becoming one of the greatest missionaries of all time.

Trace Andrew's travels from Galilee and Capernaum to the far away lands to better understand his influence on early Christianity. Find an outline map of the world or a map of the world in New Testament times. Locate Bethany, Bethsaida, Jerusalem, Greece and Scythia, the land between the Caspian Sea and the Black Sea. If the map has room, add Scotland. Andrew is considered the patron saint of Scotland, Greece and Russia. Place tracing paper over the areas where Andrew traveled. Draw an X-shaped cross in the areas he visited and write in the names. Include the old and new names of places if the map shows them. How did Andrew travel to most of the places? The traced map can be a reminder of how far some of the disciples journeyed to be "fishers of people."

RUSSIA

Supplies:
- White glue
- Tongue depressors
- Paint brushes
- Sandpaper
- Markers with fine points
- Black glossy acrylic paint
- Tacky glue

Andrew is mentioned several time in the Gospels, but later accounts of his life are very unreliable. He is associated with Scythia, now part of Russia. It is said that Andrew spread the Good News of Jesus to the people of this area. Andrew is a patron saint of Russia, as well as Greece and Scotland.

The cross is cherished by Christians everywhere as a sign of hope. St. Andrew's cross is unique in that it is a diagonal shape. In Russia, black lacquerware with brightly painted flowers is a traditional art form and adorns many crosses. Crosses may be elaborately crafted or simply constructed. Make a Saint Andrew's cross, representative of one that might be found in Russia.

Use two tongue depressors for the pieces of the cross. Lightly sand the sticks. Join the sticks together with tacky glue. Paint the sticks black on both sides and allow them to dry. Create bright flowers, leaves and vines on the front of the cross with a painted glue method. Dot white glue onto the wood in the desired shapes. Let the glue dry until it is hard and clear. Color the dried glue with fine point markers. Display the cross as a special symbol of Andrew's influence on the people of Russia.

SCOTLAND

Supplies:
- ❑ Medium blue construction paper, cut into 4" x 6" rectangles
- ❑ White paper strips, cut to 3/4" x 7"
- ❑ Scissors
- ❑ Glue sticks
- ❑ Straws or sticks
- ❑ Tape

Saint Andrew is the patron saint for Scotland as well as Greece and part of Russia. According to tradition, Andrew was crucified in Greece, on a cross of diagonal beams. The saltire, or X-shaped cross, has become the symbol for St. Andrew.

Several hundred years after Andrew's death, a monk named Regulus reached the coast of Scotland carrying some of Andrew's bones, which are called relics. Regulus settled on the east coast of Scotland and became the first bishop of the ancient town of St. Andrews. The Picts, early inhabitants of Scotland, and the English were at war at that time. Hungus, one of the kings of the Picts, had a dream in which Andrew assured him of victory. The next day during the battle, an X-shaped cross shone in the sky right over the Pict's army. The English were frightened by the shining cross and lost the war. The battle cry of the Picts was "St. Andrew, our patron, be our guide." Since that time the Scot's flag has had a white St. Andrew's cross on a field of blue, representing the shining cross in the sky.

Make a flag of Scotland as a reminder of St. Andrew's far-reaching influence. Cross two white strips diagonally and glue them onto the blue background. Clip off any of the paper strip that extends beyond the corners of the blue rectangle. Add a "flag pole" by taping a straw or stick to one side of the flag. Display the flag.

Chapter Four

James

James is the name of several different persons in the New Testament. The Hebrew form of James is Jacob, a name treasured in Hebrew tradition because Jacob was the progenitor of the twelve tribes of Israel. Since James is such a common New Testament name, there can be great confusion when searching for information about a particular person. There were even two disciples named James. The subject of this learning center is the James referred to in: Matthew 4:21; 10:2; 17:1; 20:20; 26:37; Mark 1:19-20, 29; 3:17; 5:37; 9:2; 10:35, 41; 13:3; 14:33; Luke 5:10; 6:14; 8:51; 9:28; 54; Acts 1:13; 12:2. Learn about James through experiences involving his many names, nicknames and titles: the son of Zebedee, the Greater, the son of thunder, the leader of the Jerusalem Church, the martyr and the patron saint of Spain. Explore the various aspects of James' life by participating in a learning activity for each of these "names."

JAMES THE SON OF ZEBEDEE

Supplies:
- Coffee cans
- Construction paper
- Markers
- Fabric or tissue paper
- Darning or crewel needle
- Branches
- Scissors
- Reference books and commentaries
- Ribbon, string or yarn

James, the son of Zebedee, was a fisherman on the Sea of Galilee. James and his brother, John, were in their boat mending their nets when Jesus saw them and called them to follow him (Mark 1:19-20). They, like their other fishing partners, Peter and Andrew, immediately left their father with the hired men and went to follow the Lord. In most references to the two brothers, James is mentioned first, probably because he might have been the oldest. With the exception of one incident, his martyrdom, James is never mentioned in the Bible without reference to John. Some say Salome was James' mother. She, too, was devoted to Jesus and was one of the women who witnessed the crucifixion (Matthew 27:56), and who anointed Jesus' body with spices. Some suggest that Salome was the sister of Jesus' mother, Mary. If this is true, James would have been Jesus' cousin. At any rate, James had a family who loved Jesus and sought to serve the Savior. Remember the people in James' family by making a family tree.

Disciples Then! Disciples Now! — 29

Fill a coffee can with rocks and set a small tree branch in the center of it. Decorate the can with tissue paper or fabric which has been secured in place with ribbon or yarn. Cut leaf shapes from construction paper and write the names of James and his family members on each of them. Refer to reference books and commentaries to get at the roots of James' heritage, and add additional names that are discovered. Use a needle with a large eye to thread yarn through each leaf, then hang it on a branch.

JAMES THE GREATER

Supplies:
- ❑ Bibles
- ❑ Scissors
- ❑ Brass paper fasteners
- ❑ Rulers
- ❑ Pencils
- ❑ Markers, fine-tipped
- ❑ Tape
- ❑ Heavy paper
- ❑ Circle patterns, 12" and 8" (pizza boards or paper plates)

James, the Greater, was one of the disciples in the inner circle of Jesus' closest friends, along with Peter and John. The title, "the Greater," was added to distinguish this man from another disciple who was the son of Alphaeus and who was known as James, "the Less." In the Bible, the descriptive terms "greater" or "less" may refer to size or age, not importance.

James, the Greater, must have been very close to Jesus, because he witnessed several significant events including the raising of Jairus' daughter, the transfiguration of Jesus on the mountain, the healing of Peter's mother-in-law and the agony of Jesus at the Garden of Gethsemane. The Bible tells us very little about the life of James; however, historians report of his influence in the beginning of the early Christian church. Construct a circle reminder to illustrate some important occasions in the life of Jesus which included James, the Greater.

Using the larger pattern, trace and cut two circles from the heavy paper. Trace and cut out the small circle, then mark lines dividing it into fourths. In each of the sections, draw a picture illustrating the scenes witnessed by James.

Use the Bible to discover what happened in the following passages:
- Jesus raising Jairus' daughter: Mark 5:35-43
- Jesus' transfigurations: Matthew 17:1-9; Mark 9:2-8
- Jesus praying at Gethsemane: Matthew 26:36-46
- Jesus healing Peter's mother-in-law: Mark 1:29-31

Take one of the large circles for the inside layer of the Bible verse viewer. Cut a two inch slit into the circle and continue around the outside until you have cut away a curved strip about six inches long. This forms a viewing window.

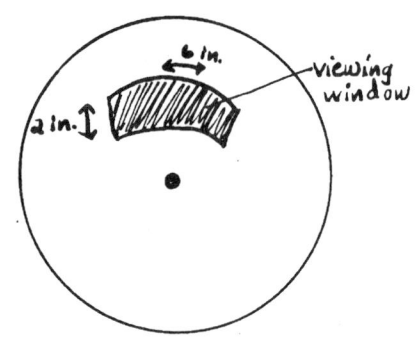

On the outside edge of the remaining circle, write the four scripture passages, spacing them five or six inches apart. You may choose to copy several lines from the Bible descriptions to go with each illustration. Be sure the writing fits within the open area of the viewing window.

Assemble the viewer by stacking the circles in this order: on the bottom, the piece with the written verses, next the "window" piece, and on top, the small circle displaying the pictures. Carefully punch a brass paper fastener into the center of the stacked circles and secure the fastener behind the bottom piece.

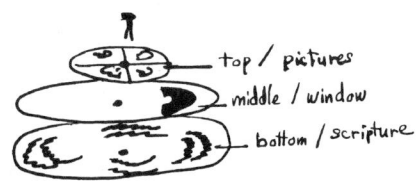

Turn the bottom circle to display writing, then rotate the small circle until the picture and verse match. Share this viewer with someone who does not know about the disciple James, the Greater.

JAMES THE SON OF THUNDER

Supplies:

- ❏ Paper
- ❏ Book of names
- ❏ Pencils
- ❏ Weather page from newspaper

Jesus gave several of the disciples new names when they became his followers; some were given nicknames. James and his brother John were called the "sons of thunder," which could have referred to their impetuous behavior, their tremendous eloquence, their powerful voices, their fiery temperament or their zeal and dedication to the Lord. What other reasons might Jesus have had for calling James a "son of thunder"? Read Mark 10:35. James and his brother, John, had a bold request for Jesus. They asked to be seated on his right and left in glory.

Disciples Then! Disciples Now! — 31

Choosing a name for a new baby is an important event for families. Many times a child is given the name of a favorite relative or friend; in other instances, a name having a special meaning is chosen. Nicknames are informal names which may describe personality or appearance. What do you know about your name?

Look through a baby book or book of names to determine what your name means. Write your full name across the top of a sheet of paper, then fold the paper into fourths. In one section write the meaning of your name, then next to it write a few sentences explaining why your name was selected.

Do you have a nickname? In the third part of the folded paper, explain what your nickname is, and in the fourth, how it came to be.

Jesus helps us understand what James was like by using the word "thunder" in his nickname. What weather term would help people know a little more about you? Are you the "daughter of sunshine" or the "son of clouds"? Think of all types of weather words, then pick one that describes you. In the last section of the paper, write your weather word and why you selected it.

Post the name sheet on the bulletin board with others from the class and learn "what's in a name".

JAMES THE LEADER OF THE JERUSALEM CHURCH

Supplies:
- Paper
- Pens

After the day of Pentecost, James the disciple of Jesus took on a new name, or title. He became a leader of the Jerusalem Church until his martyrdom. It is estimated that James was a leader of the band of believers for twelve to fourteen years.

Think about the qualities that are needed by a leader. Take a piece of paper and write the word "L E A D E R" vertically down the left side of the sheet. Write a word describing the qualities of a leader that begins with each of the letters. For example:

L ove
E nergy
A ffirmation
D ecision making
E mpathy
R esources

What gifts of leadership can you use for Jesus? Try writing the acrostic poem again, describing your own gifts for each letter.

JAMES THE MARTYR

Supplies:
- Glass casters
- Pictures of anchors
- Cardboard
- Tacky glue or glue gun
- Clear tape
- Paper
- Scissors
- Felt
- Markers

The report of the death of James is recorded in Acts 12:1-2. James defended his faith and was beheaded for what he believed. He was the first disciple to become a martyr — someone who is put to death or tortured because of religious or other beliefs. James is the only disciple whose death is mentioned in the Bible. This brief sentence in Acts 12 is the only time James is mentioned alone, or without his brother John, in the scriptures.

Would you be as brave as James? How will you "stand up" for what you believe? Make a paperweight with an anchor to represent "holding fast" to your faith.

Glass casters are small, shallow containers placed under furniture legs to protect floors or carpets. They are usually round and made of heavy, clear glass. Glass casters can also be turned into paperweights. Choose a picture of an anchor or draw an original one with markers and paper. Center the caster over the drawing, then trace and cut around it. Trim a thin strip of paper from around the outside edge.

Place the caster in front of you with the flat side down on the table. Fit the anchor illustration into the bottom of the caster with the picture facing down. Be certain the paper fits snugly. Tiny pieces of tape will help hold it in place. Trace and cut the cardboard circle to cover the opening. For a finished look, glue a piece of felt onto the bottom.

Turn over the glass to view the anchor symbol. Enjoy the paperweight as a reminder to stand up for your beliefs and to hold fast to your faith.

place image face down in caster opening. Add cardboard and cover with felt.

JAMES THE PATRON SAINT OF SPAIN

Supplies:
- ❑ Cardboard or mats (the kind used inside picture frames)
- ❑ Tacky glue or glue gun and glue sticks
- ❑ Shells, assorted sizes
- ❑ Photograph of each participant
- ❑ Construction paper
- ❑ Scissors
- ❑ Mat knife
- ❑ Ruler
- ❑ Pencil
- ❑ Tape

Legends tell us that James, the brother of John, was the first missionary to carry the Gospel to Spain. Many believe that after James was killed in Jerusalem, his body was buried in Spain where the Cathedral of Santiago de Compostela now stands. A lot of information about the disciples comes from historians. People who study the Bible and the history surrounding it sometimes disagree on the events which are not recorded in scripture.

We do know for certain that the apostle James is the patron saint of Spain, but during the middle ages, the Cathedral of Santiago de Compostela was an important site for pilgrimages.

The familiar symbol for James includes three scallop shells, which represent his missionary journeys. Sometimes James is symbolized by a single scallop shell and a sword, which depicts the way he died. Christians on pilgrimages during the middle ages fastened shells to their clothing. Decorate a picture frame with shells, then use it to display a photograph of yourself. This will be reminder that you, as well as James, can be a missionary by sharing Jesus' teachings.

Select a piece of cardboard or a mat to fit the photograph. To form a mat, mark the cardboard and carefully cut an opening a little smaller than the photo.

Use caution when cutting with a mat knife, and protect the table with an extra piece of cardboard. Select enough shells to cover the mat. Glue the shells in place. When the glue is dry, tape the photo to the back of the frame. Cut a piece of construction paper to fit the back of the frame. Glue the paper in place to protect the photo.

Give the framed photograph to someone special and share what you have learned about the disciple, James.

Chapter Five

John

John, the brother of James and the son of Zebedee, was one of the disciples closest to Jesus. John was probably the "beloved disciple" referred to in the book of John. This special man was with Jesus on the momentous occasions of his transfiguration and his agony in Gethsemane. Tradition has connected John with the unnamed "disciple whom Jesus loved," who leaned on his Master's breast at the Last Supper, to whom Jesus on the cross confided the care of his mother, who ran before Peter to the tomb on the morning of the resurrection and, seeing it empty, believed. It was John who first recognized the risen Lord by the Sea of Tiberias. The fourth Gospel, three biblical epistles and the book of Revelation traditionally bear the name of St. John as their author.

Share the story of John, the man and his mission, through involvement in seven learning center activities related to his life and work. Participants will come to learn that John "heard the Word," "shared the Word," "responded to the Word," "spoke the Word," "wrote the Word" and "reflected the Word," and that they must "remember the Word".

JOHN HEARD THE WORD

Supplies:
- Bibles
- Blank tape(s)
- Paper
- Markers
- Tape recorder
- Earphones
- Pens

One of the meanings of the word "hear" is to be informed of or to be told of or about. Most likely John heard about Jesus in many ways. His parents, Zebedee and Salome, were followers of Jesus. John and his brother James, together with their fishing partners Simon Peter and Andrew, were most likely early disciples of John the Baptist, the New Testament prophet who foretold the coming of the Messiah. One day while John and James were in the boat with their father mending fishing nets, John heard the call of Jesus to "Follow him." Immediately, the biblical account reports, John left the boat and followed Jesus.

Review the passages in the Bible that refer to ways in which John heard about Jesus and listened to Jesus' call to become a disciple. Scripture verses include Luke 5:1-11; Mark 1:19-20; Matthew 4:18-22. Read the passages into a tape recorder. Once they are recorded, play them back and listen to John's story.

On a piece of paper, use a pen or marker and write or draw at least five ways in which you have heard about Jesus. Ideas include: reading the Bible, going to church school, listening to parents, watching a Bible story video and talking with a friend.

JOHN SHARED THE WORD

Supplies:
- Church school leaflets depicting Bible-times people
- Bible
- Pencils
- Tape
- Cardboard or cardstock
- Glue
- Drawing paper
- Markers or Crayons
- Scissors
- Tongue depressors or craft sticks

The disciple John, his brother James and their fishing partner, Peter, formed the inner circle of Jesus' closest friends. These three were present during the significant events in the life and ministry of Jesus. John witnessed many miracles performed by Jesus, but chose to write about the certain "signs" which best explained the true nature of the Son of God. John shares the Word with us as he emphasizes the meaning of the happening instead of just the facts.

John's writings highlight the following miracles: John 2:1-11, turning water to wine; John 4:46-54, healing the official's son; John 5:1-18, healing on the Sabbath; John 6:1-14, feeding the five thousand; John 6:16-21, walking on water; John 9:1-7, curing the blind man and John 11:38-44, raising Lazarus from the dead. Read these accounts in the book of John and choose one to illustrate. Create a simple rod puppet to complete a mini-theater and to act out the dramatic event.

After reading the accounts listed above, illustrate one of the miracles John observed and shared with us in his writings recorded in the Bible. Make large and colorful drawings of the persons and the place involved in the story. Be sure to include details to tell more about the setting for the event...was it at the sea, in a building, or at a special gathering?

When the drawing is finished, use the ruler and pencil to draw a line across the bottom of the paper, approximately two inches up from the bottom and one inch in from each side. Turn the drawing over and put tape across the area where the line was marked. Additional tape above and below the line will help reinforce the paper. Carefully cut along the strengthened line to form a slot at the bottom of the drawing. Set the illustration aside.

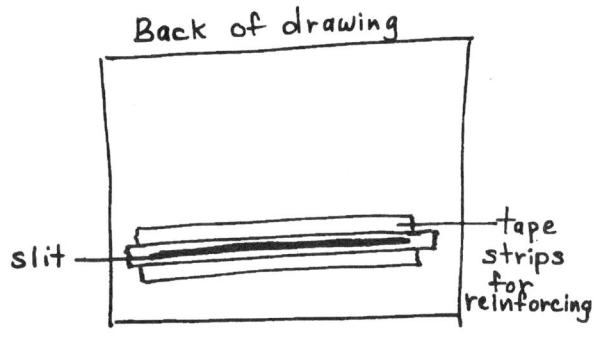

Form the simple rod puppet by drawing a picture of John or Jesus on the cardstock. Cut out the shape and tape it to a stick. Be sure to keep the figure size similar to those in the drawing. If church school leaflet pictures are available, cut out a person and glue it to cardstock. Trim away excess paper.

Use care to slide the puppet into the slot. Act out the story of the miracle by moving the puppet back and forth through the scene.

Share the Word using the mini-theater to tell the miracle story to family and friends.

JOHN RESPONDED TO THE WORD

Supplies:
- ❏ Bibles
- ❏ Pens or pencils
- ❏ Paper

Since the Gospel of John was written that men might believe that Jesus Christ is God, the son of the Father, it is understandable that there are several accounts of persons who responded to prove this fact. John's own response to Jesus is recorded in the book, too. Unscramble the names of seven of the people who acknowledged Jesus as the son of God. Use the scripture references as an aid in deciphering the words. Look up the verses and read the statement of faith made by each person. The names and verses to use are:

- SHMOAT — John 20:28 [Thomas]
- EERPT — John 6:69 [Peter]
- TJTOHAEPBTHNSI — John 1:34 [John The Baptist]
- NJHO — John 20:31 [John]
- TCSIRH — John 10:36 [Christ]
- TAHAMR — John 11:27 [Martha]
- TALEANAHN — John 1:49 [Nathanael]

Continue the activity by using the letters of the alphabet to write a faith response in the form of an ABC poem. ABC poetry is written in a short form and

Disciples Then! Disciples Now!

expresses strong emotion. The first four lines are clauses expressing emotion or stating information. The initial letters of the beginning words in each line are written alphabetically. The first line does not have to begin with A, however. Line five is a sentence starting with any letter. For example:

B ible stories tell me about Jesus
C hrist, the son of God.
D ied to give me
E ternal life.
I believe!

Use the paper and pens or pencils and create a personal poem. Post the results and invite other learners to read the creative writing project.

JOHN SPOKE THE WORD

Supplies:
- Bible
- Nutcracker and nutpick
- Scissors
- Paper strips
- Narrow ribbon or yarn
- Walnuts in the shell
- Magnet strip
- Pen or fine-tipped markers
- Glue gun or tacky glue

"In the beginning was the Word, and the Word was with God, and the Word was God." Those beautiful words spoken to Christians at Ephesus became the opening of the Gospel according to John. John lived and preached for many years in Jerusalem, he traveled to Samaria with Peter and later, he was sent in exile to the Isle of Patmos off the coast of Greece. After many years, he was allowed to rejoin the followers at Ephesus in Asia Minor, where he continued to speak and write about Jesus. John is known for emphasizing what Jesus said rather than what he did. Some of the most beloved verses of scripture come from the book of John. The verse that is sometimes called the "Gospel in a nutshell" is John 3:16: "For God so loved the world that He gave His only son, so that everyone who believes in him may not perish but may have eternal life."

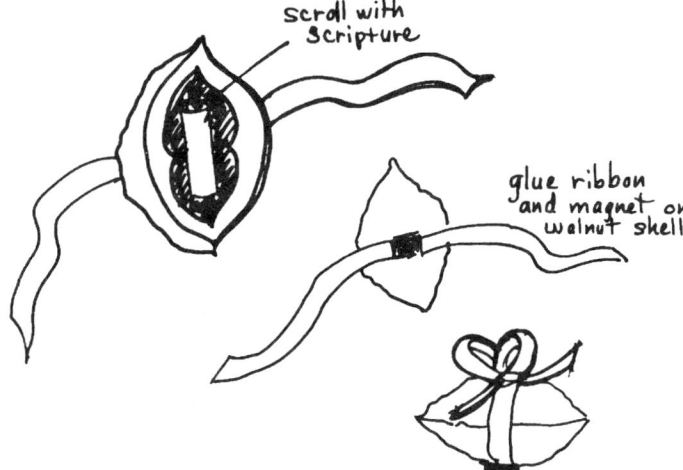

Make a magnet reminder of the "Gospel in a nutshell". Carefully crack open a walnut, keeping the two halves intact; then pick out the nut meats. The nut meats may be eaten or set aside. Glue about eight inches of ribbon or yarn width-wise to the outside of one of the nut halves. Attach the magnet and set the piece aside so the glue can dry.

Find John 3:16 in the Bible and copy the verse onto a paper strip. Roll the strip into a tiny scroll and place it inside the nutshell which has the glued magnet.

Fit the two halves together to enclose the scroll, then tie a bow around the "lid" to hold the shells securely.

Memorize the verse inside the nutshell so you can "speak" about the Gospel as John did. Give away the magnet or place it somewhere as a reminder of Jesus' teachings.

JOHN WROTE THE WORD

Supplies:
- ❑ Bibles
- ❑ Pencils
- ❑ Markers
- ❑ Manila file folders
- ❑ Scissors
- ❑ Envelopes

Although there is some dispute among biblical scholars about the authorship of the Gospel of John, the epistles I, II and III John and the book of Revelation, John is generally credited with writing them. John wrote to prove that Jesus was the Christ, the promised Messiah for the Jews and the son of God for the Gentiles, and to lead readers to believe in the second person of the Trinity as their personal savior. In fact, the word "believe" is used ninety-eight times in the Gospel. It is interesting to note that the deity of Jesus Christ is revealed in every chapter of the book of John. Explore these verses in an interesting, involving format. Create a jigsaw puzzle by writing scripture passages on the pieces, and use this game to learn more about the deity of Jesus.

Select a manila file folder and cut it into twenty-one jigsaw puzzle pieces. If desired, draw the shapes on the heavy paper before cutting them apart. Write one of the following scripture verses on each puzzle piece: John 1:49; 2:11; 3:16; 4:26; 5:25; 6:33; 7:37; 8:58; 9:37; 10:30; 11:27; 12:32; 13:13; 14:1; 15:5; 16:7; 17:1; 18:37; 19:30; 20:28; 21:22. Mix up the pieces. Select one shape at a time and look up the verse in the Bible. Read the scripture passage and reflect on the way it illustrates that Jesus is the son of God and the savior of the world. Write or draw a word or picture on the blank side of the puzzle piece to serve as a reminder of the content or theme of the verse. For example, for John 15:5 a vine may be drawn, or for John 20:28 the word "Thomas" might be written. Continue the process until the puzzle is reassembled.

Put the puzzle pieces in a envelope and take them home to share the activity with a family member or friend.

JOHN REFLECTED THE WORD

Supplies:
- ❑ Large letter stencils or patterns for J, O, H, N
- ❑ Construction paper, 12" x 18"
- ❑ Markers
- ❑ Paper scraps
- ❑ Glue or glue sticks
- ❑ Pencils
- ❑ Scissors
- ❑ Magazines
- ❑ Bible

John reflected the words of the Gospel in his life and in his interpretation of the teachings of Jesus. He is known as "the beloved disciple," and love is a major theme in his writings. Another main theme is light, and his contributions to the Bible shed light on the true nature of Jesus.

A traditional symbol for the shield of John features a serpent and a chalice. Legends tell that a pagan priest planned to kill John with poisoned wine. After the disciple made the sign of the cross over the drink, the poison turned into a snake and crawled out of the chalice. He drank the wine and was not harmed. Another story states that John was arrested in Rome and was condemned to death by Emperor Domitian. John was plunged into a cauldron of boiling oil, but escaped unharmed. The Emperor then sent him away to the Isle of Patmos. Both of these stories remind us that John was spared from dying a martyr's death. He is reported to be the only disciple to die peacefully at an old age. In addition to the cauldron or serpent and chalice, the eagle is a common symbol attributed to St. John, the Evangelist. The eagle represents the "soaring upward" or the inspiration in his writings.

Design a name collage using words and symbols to describe the beloved disciple, John. Select a favorite color of construction paper and place it horizontally on the working space. Trace patterns for the letters that spell "JOHN." Center the word so the finished collage will be more attractive. Decorate the letters J, H and N by coloring in solid or by adding dots or stripes.

The "O" in the name collage will contain words and symbols which portray something about this disciple. Fill in the circle shape with words such as "Love" or "Light" which have been cut from magazines or paper scraps. Cut or draw the symbols associated with John. Look in the Bible to find favorite verses from the writings of the disciple and add those to the collage. Glue or draw words and symbols neatly inside the outline of the "O" in John's name design. The pieces of the collage can be placed in sections marked off in the circle or can be arranged

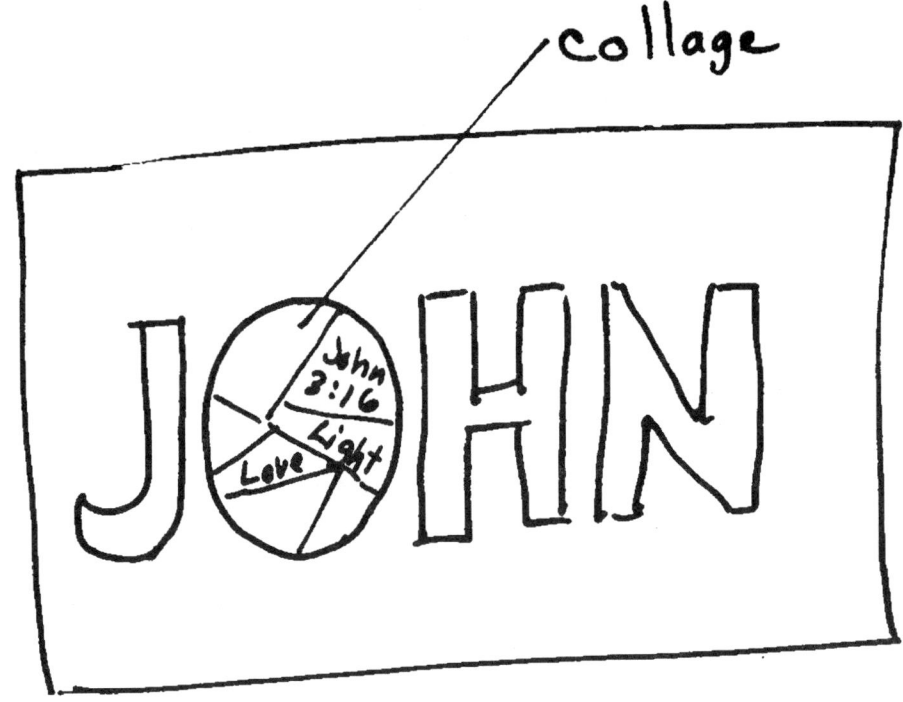

casually. Display the name designs and be able to explain to others how the writings and symbols reflect the "WORD" as well as the life and death of Jesus.

WE REMEMBER THE WORD

Supplies:
- Bibles
- Construction paper
- Scissors
- Patterns for hearts and circles
- Pencils
- Markers
- String
- Hole punch and tape

John the disciple was probably Jesus' closest friend, and is referred to as the beloved disciple. John traveled and taught until he was an old man. In his old age, Christian friends encouraged him to write down what he remembered about Jesus. He remembered being with Jesus on the mountain top, at Gethsemane and at the Crucifixion. More than some of the other disciples, he remembered Jesus' words.

John is sometimes called the Apostle of Love because of the themes of love in his writings. It is recorded that he is also known as the Apostle of Childhood because of the following words attributed to him several times in I John: "Little children, love one another."

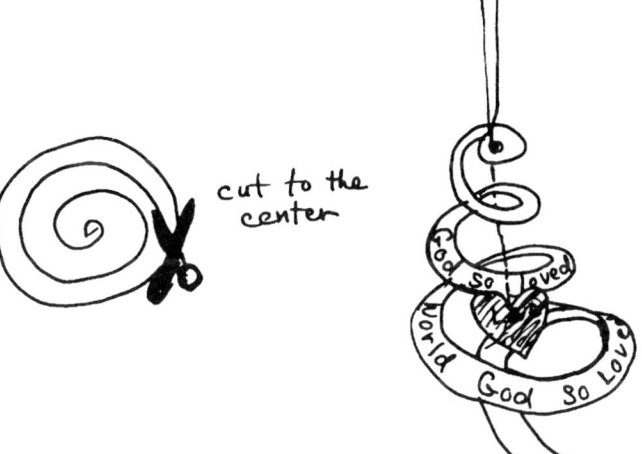

Create a mobile with words from the writings of John or the words he remembered hearing Jesus say. Find a scripture verse from John's writings with the message of love: God so loved the world; God is Love; Little children, love one another. Write it on a scrap of paper and put it aside. Trace and cut out a heart and a circle, approximately 8 inches in diameter. Change the circle into a spiral by cutting from the outer edge, following the shape until the scissors reaches the center.

Write the selected verse along the spiral strip. Punch a hole in the center portion of the spiral and at the top of the heart. Use tape to reinforce the paper before punching the hole if the paper is thin. Write the word "Love" with decorative lettering in the center of the heart on both sides. Cut yarn about eighteen inches long and thread it through the hole in the heart and in the spiral. Tie a knot in the yarn and arrange the spiral so it surrounds the heart.

Hang the mobile as a symbol of love. Memorize the words and share the message with a least one other person!

Chapter Six

Philip

Although there is little information about the life of the disciple Philip, we do know that he was a person who asked questions, and a man who had questions asked of him. Since Philip was from Bethsaida, he could have been a fisherman, and most likely, he was a follower of John the Baptist. After Jesus asked Philip to "Follow," Philip went to tell his friend Nathanael, also called Bartholomew, that he had found the Messiah. When Nathanael asked, "Can any good thing come out of Nazareth?" Philip replied with the simple statement: "Come and see." There are many other questions involved in the story of Philip. Jesus asked Philip how the crowd of 5000 could be fed; the Greeks asked Philip for an audience with Jesus; Philip asked Jesus how he could know God. There are questions about the accuracy of the accounts of Philip's later life. Activities in six learning centers are designed to help participants learn more about Jesus' disciple Philip. Each learning center focuses on one of the questions related to Philip's story.

WHO IS PHILIP?

Supplies:

❏ Paper ❏ Pens, pencils, markers
❏ Bibles ❏ Folder

Begin the study of Philip's life by reviewing several scripture passages: John 1:43-46; John 6:1-7; John 12:22; John 14:8-10. After reading the verses, write a rebus story about all or part of Philip's life. A rebus story is one which includes pictures or symbols to suggest words and phrases. Take a piece of paper and a writing tool and tell the story in this unique way. Draw a person representing Philip to use throughout the narrative instead of writing his name. Each time the picture occurs, read the word "Philip." Make a question mark instead of writing the word "question" each time Philip asks or answers an inquiry. Make the story any length, and include as much description and detail as desired. Put your name on the paper and place it in the folder so other participants may review the rebus accounts and learn about the life of Philip.

"CAN ANYTHING GOOD COME OUT OF NAZARETH?"

Supplies:
- ❏ Hand mirror or small mirror hanging near work area
- ❏ Drawing paper, good quality white or cream
- ❏ Drawing pencil, soft-lead ❏ Soft eraser
- ❏ Construction paper ❏ Scissors
- ❏ Glue sticks ❏ Bible

Philip is named as the fifth in the list of apostles. Born at Bethsaida, he was probably a fisherman like Peter, Andrew, James and John. Jesus met Philip at Galilee and simply called him by saying, "Follow me." Philip, in turn, summoned his friend Nathanael to see the Messiah. Nathanael seemed skeptical when he asked, "Can anything good come out of Nazareth?" There must have been something sincere and convincing in Philip's manner which persuaded Nathanael, for he followed when his friend said, "Come and see." (John 1:43-46)

Consider these questions: What did these men, some who were strangers, see in Jesus' face to cause them to stop everything and follow him? What did the faces of Andrew and Philip show that convinced Simon Peter and Nathanael to "come and see?" What might people see in you that would make them want to follow Jesus?

Using a mirror, look carefully at yourself, then use a pencil to draw your self-portrait onto a piece of paper. Carefully study your face as you look into the mirror. What is the general shape of your face? Lightly sketch the outline and add the lines for neck and shoulders. Keep pencil lines light so they can be easily erased without smudging or tearing the paper. Eyes will be approximately in the middle of the face outline—allowing for nose, mouth and chin below and keeping space for brow and hair above. Look closely at the shape of the eyes and the curve of the mouth, because these features determine expression. Add details that make you unique, such as glasses, freckles, dimples, smile and frown lines. Darken the pencil lines when you are satisfied with the results.

Use the construction paper to make a frame for your self-portrait. Cut an oval or rectangular opening, then glue the frame over the drawing to show off the face. What qualities about that special face might encourage someone to believe you when you talk about Jesus? Could it be a sincere smile, kind eyes or an expression of enthusiasm? Display the completed self-portrait with other portraits of "disciples" from the class.

"WHERE ARE WE TO BUY BREAD FOR THESE PEOPLE TO EAT?"

Supplies:
- ❏ Copies or outline drawings of Philip's symbol
- ❏ Unbleached muslin squares, 16" x 16"

- ❏ Scissors
- ❏ Pencils
- ❏ White paper
- ❏ Heat resistant pad or iron rest
- ❏ Fabric crayons
- ❏ Newspaper
- ❏ Iron
- ❏ Darning needle or hat pin

Advance Preparation:
- Follow directions on crayon package when purchasing fabric. Some fabric crayons work best on cloth that is 50% cotton and 50% polyester, but check the instructions to be certain. Fabric may be laundered, cut to size and hemmed before placing it in the activity center. Recruit an adult to guide the ironing.

As Jesus went around the sea of Galilee healing the sick, a large crowd began following Him. He and his disciples went up to the mountain to rest as the group came toward them. Jesus asked Philip, "Where are we to buy bread for these people to eat?" Philip, being a practical man, answered that he did not think it was possible to feed such a large crowd. The disciple did not consider that Jesus was testing him. (John 6:1-7)

The five loaves and two fishes provided by a small boy were used to feed the five thousand people who had gathered. After the "miraculous lunch," the people said, "This is indeed the prophet who is to come into the world." (John 6:14) The most familiar symbol for Philip includes a Latin cross and loaves of bread. The loaves are a reminder that Philip was present at the feeding of the multitude and the cross represents the disciple's faith journey.

Design a bread basket liner including the traditional symbol attributed to Philip. Each time the bread cloth is used, remember one of Jesus' miracles and his disciple Philip.

Older children may enjoy fringing the edges of the cloth. The fringed edge is formed by pulling threads one at a time until about one inch is frayed or unraveled. Continue until all sides are fringed. A darning needle or hat pin will help to free individual threads from the woven cloth.

Trace or draw the cross and loaves symbol onto the white paper and color with fabric crayons.

color with fabric crayon on paper

Position the colored emblem, waxy side down, on one of the corners of the muslin square.

Place the drawing and cloth on the newspaper pad. Cover the emblem with clean paper, then press with a downward motion with a warm iron (follow directions for proper heat setting) until the design transfers to the muslin. Do not slide the iron back and forth.

Other lines or details may be added to embellish the bread basket liner. Just be sure to draw the design on paper first and then transfer the crayon. Be aware that any lettering or image will be reversed when the design is pressed onto the fabric.

Most fabric crayon can be washed in cold water without fading the bright colors.

Enjoy the specially designed bread basket liner at family gatherings or give it as a gift to someone. Be prepared to explain the meaning of the symbols appearing on the cloth.

HOW CAN WE SEE JESUS?

Supplies:
- ❑ Paper
- ❑ Bibles
- ❑ Pens or pencils

Although Philip was Hebrew, his name is Greek. During Holy Week some Greeks who had come to celebrate the Passover went to Philip with a request to see Jesus. Because of his Greek name, they probably assumed that Philip spoke Greek, and that he would have an approving attitude toward them. Unsure what to do, Philip went to his Greek-speaking friend, the disciple Andrew, and together they approached Jesus with the visitor's petition. Read John 12:20-26.

Imagine that you have the opportunity to have an audience with Jesus. What would you ask him? What questions might you have? What would you discuss? Take a piece of paper and a pen or pencil and write down one or more of the questions that you would like to ask Jesus. Take the paper with you, and consider sharing it with an adult whose faith you admire. This person might be a pastor, teacher, parent or friend.

"DO YOU NOT BELIEVE THAT I AM IN THE FATHER AND THE FATHER IS IN ME?"

Supplies:
- Heavy, white drawing paper
- Containers with water
- Watercolor paint boxes
- Bibles
- Cross pattern
- Candle stubs, light-colored
- Brushes
- Newspapers
- Rulers

Jesus had been outlining coming events to his disciples and had been informing them how to find, see and know the Father when Philip said, "Lord, show us the Father, and we will be satisfied." Jesus explained that he had been in their midst a long time, and since they knew the savior, they knew God as well. (John 14:1-12)

It seemed that Philip was looking for a practical answer to his request to know more about God. Jesus explained that anyone working with him the length of time Philip had should not say, "Show us the Father," but should know that they were one in the same!

Think about these questions: Do you miss the obvious when you look for God? Are you looking for the wrong characteristics? Do you look for a rational, practical explanation and discount divine power? God is with us at all times, even when we do not see clearly. As our faith and understanding develop, we are able to see and know God.

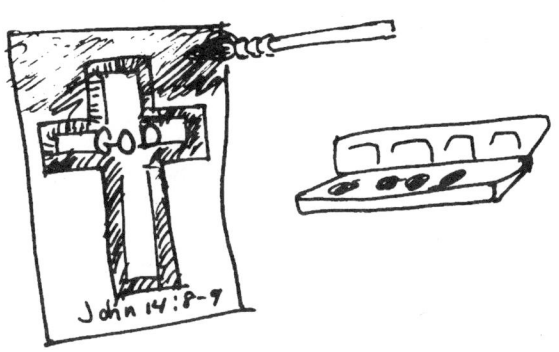

Place a piece of drawing paper vertically in front of you and draw or trace a large cross in the center. Use heavy pressure when writing or drawing with the candle stub to ensure a waxy line. Design the outline of the cross any way you choose, adding the word "GOD" to the inside of the symbol. At the bottom or side of the page, write John 14:8-9 or John 14:10. Bold printing will be easier to read. When you are certain that all symbols and words are waxy, wash over the page with a brush full of clear water. Then load the brush with color and gently paint across the markings. You may prefer to use one color for the entire page or a new color for each section. Try more than one design—just be sure "GOD" is the central part of each plan!

Disciples Then! Disciples Now!

Prepare one of the designs without painting over it and allow a friend or family member to "discover 'God' in the cross" when he or she uses the paint wash technique.

WHAT HAPPENED TO PHILIP?

Supplies:
- Scissors
- Pencils
- Paper scraps, contrasting colors
- Glue
- Construction paper, 1/2" x 24"
- Circle pattern

Philip the disciple and apostle of Jesus is often confused with Philip the evangelist mentioned in the book of Acts. The later Philip was one of the seven chosen to assist the Twelve. Philip the evangelist was a successful missionary in Samaria (Acts 6:1-6), was instrumental in the conversion of the Ethiopian eunuch (Acts 8:26-40) and hosted Paul in Caesarea (Acts 2:7-10). Since Peter and John had to go to Samaria to put their blessing on the work of Philip the evangelist, we can be quite certain that this person was not Philip the apostle, who had already been given authority to preach and teach in Jesus' name. Philip the disciple is mentioned in the book of Acts only as having been present in the upper room (1:13) and at Pentecost (2:1-7). Legends tell us that Philip was one of the leaders of the Christian movement in Asia. Accounts of Philip's death vary greatly. Some traditions maintain that Philip was martyred at Hierapolis, another claims that he was crucified, still another says he was hanged, and one states that he died of natural causes. Regardless of the accuracy of any of these accounts, there is one thing that cannot be questioned: Philip knew, loved and served Jesus.

Make a bookmark and use it as a reminder of the story of Philip. Choose a long piece of construction paper. Measure 10 1/2" from one end and use a pencil to mark it lightly. Using the mark for a guide, fold the strip at a 90° angle. Fold the long remaining end of the strip so that it is parallel to the first side. This will make a point where the folds meet. Trace and cut the circle from a small piece of paper. Carefully cut a slit in the center of the circle. Pull the pointed end of the folded strip through the slit. Draw a question mark shape on a contrasting piece of paper and cut it out. Glue the question mark onto the place where the strips and the slit in the circle come together. Other materials may be used to make the bookmarks, such as heavy cloth that does not ravel, felt or leather pieces.

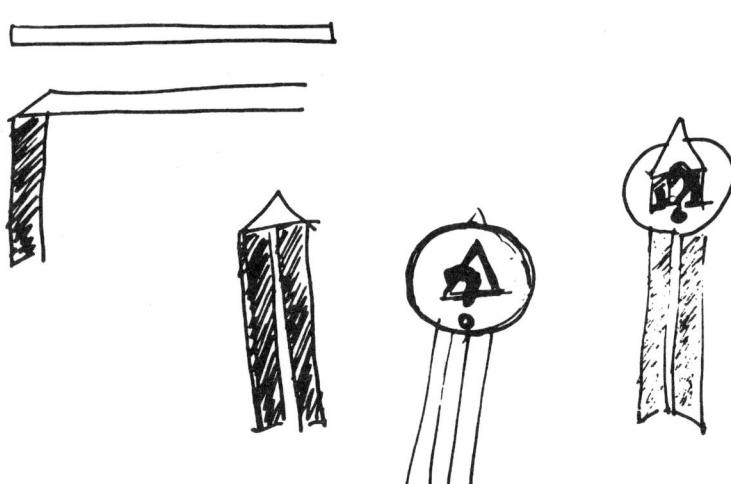

Put the bookmark in your Bible to mark one of your favorite passages about the life of Philip. When people ask what the question mark represents, tell the story of Philip using the questions in the story as the outline. Remember that Philip had no questions when it came to the fact that Jesus was the Messiah!

Chapter Seven

Bartholomew

One of Jesus' disciples is referred to by the name Bartholomew in the Gospels of Matthew, Mark and Luke, and by the name Nathanael in the book of John. It is thought that Nathanael was the man's given name, and that Bartholomew was his family name. Although there is a wonderful story about Nathanael Bartholomew's introduction to Jesus by his friend and fellow disciple, Philip, there is not much more known about this man chosen by Jesus to spread the news of the savior. From the brief scripture stories, primarily recorded in John 1:45-51, as well as from traditions and histories, we do know that Bartholomew was a son, friend, student, witness and missionary. Learning center activities are developed for these five themes. Use the information and ideas provided to discover ways in which Bartholomew was a disciple then, and ways in which you can follow his example now!

BARTHOLOMEW AS A SON

Supplies:
- ❏ Sheets of self-stick labels, at least 2 1/2 inches by 3 1/2 inches
- ❏ Permanent markers, fine-tipped black plus colors
- ❏ Pencils   ❏ Rulers
- ❏ Scratch paper

How many names do you have? Family members, friends and teachers may refer to you in a different manner. For example, a man named William Jones might be known as William, Willie, Bill, Billy, Jones, Jonesy or Mr. Jones. Sometimes people will say, "Bill Jones from Main Street," or "Bill Jones, the son of John Jones."

Several of Jesus' disciples are known by two names. One of them is a man called Bartholomew and Nathanael. In the books of Matthew, Mark and Luke the name Bartholomew appears in the list of disciples; in the book of John it seems that Nathanael is the same person as Bartholomew. Most likely, Nathanael is the apostle's first name. His parents must have been very happy when he was born, because in Hebrew his name means "Gift of God" or "God has Given." The disciple also was known by his last name, Bartholomew, derived from Bar-Talmai, which means Son of Talmai.

There is very little written in the scriptures about Bartholomew, but he seemed to be a thinker and a student. Some historians believe he was well

Disciples Then! Disciples Now! — 49

educated and possibly the only apostle of noble birth. We imagine that Bartholomew studied from scrolls recording the religious traditions and laws, just as you read the Bible. Your Bible probably has a name-plate in the front with your name and the date it was presented. In this activity, create original name-plates to be used in a Bible or other favorite books.

Decide which of your names needs to appear on the book-plates. Using scratch paper and pencil, experiment with lettering styles and symbols that best represent you. With light pencil lines, sketch plans onto the labels and mark guidelines to ensure even lettering. Repeat the design on each label or try several different ideas. Finish the decorated labels with permanent markers. Take the labels with you and personalize special books with the original name plates.

BARTHOLOMEW AS A FRIEND

Supplies:
- Index cards
- Pencils
- Paper cups
- Drinking straws or unsharpened pencils
- Markers
- Tape or glue
- Bible

In John 1:43-51, Jesus calls Philip of Bethsaida to "Follow him." Once Philip accepts the invitation, he finds his friend Nathanael Bartholomew and asks him to follow Jesus, too. Nathanael is not sure how to respond and asks Philip the question, "Can anything good come out of Nazareth?" Philip encourages him to "Come and see." When Jesus saw Nathanael walking toward him, he said, "Here is truly an Israelite in whom there is no guile." That meant a person in whom there is nothing false. Jesus did not say that Bartholomew was a person without sin, but that he was a man of high integrity, sincerity and commitment to God. Nathanael was surprised that Jesus already knew about him, and even more startled when Jesus told him that he had seen Bartholomew under the fig tree. Bartholomew proclaimed that Jesus was truly the son of God, the king of Israel. Because of a friend's invitation, Bartholomew was led to know the Lord.

Make a simple pop-up puppet to represent Bartholomew, and if desired, one to represent Philip, too. On an index card, use markers to draw a picture of Bartholomew. Color it and cut it out. Tape or glue the cut-out shape to the end of a drinking straw or to the top of an unsharpened pencil. Poke a hole in the center of the bottom of a paper cup. Insert the pencil or straw through the cup so that the cut-out figure is inside the cup and the rod extends through the bottom. Operate the puppet by moving the rod up and down so the figure pops out of the top of the cup.

Look up the passages about Bartholomew and pop up the puppet to show times when he showed his faith in Jesus, and times when he questioned it. Pop up the puppet to mean "Yes," and leave it in the cup to mean "No." If two pop-up puppets are made, pop-up the person speaking and leave the other in the cup.

BARTHOLOMEW AS A STUDENT

Supplies:
- Posterboard
- Markers or crayons
- Paper punch
- Magazines, newspapers or used church school papers
- Scissors
- Glue
- Yarn, string or ribbon.

Bartholomew's name suggests that he may have been a special kind of student. "Bar" means son, so Bartholomew was probably "Son of Talmai." This was a noble name at the time of Jesus. A <u>tholmai</u> was highly regarded in Hebrew circles as a leader of scripture study, and Bartholomew may have been one of the special students of that school. In John 1:45 Philip tells Nathanael Bartholomew, "We have found the one Moses wrote about in the Law, and about whom the prophets also wrote." This suggests that Philip and Nathanael had studied the Law and the prophets together.

In the story of Bartholomew's first encounter with Jesus, our Lord said: "I saw you while you were still under the fig tree before Philip called you." (John 1:48) The fig tree was and continues to be a favorite tree in Israel. It normally grows to be about fifteen feet in height, with an expanse of branches that offers shade and privacy for meditation. Rabbis and students of the scriptures thought of the fig tree as a suitable place for their study. According to tradition, when Jesus saw him under the fig tree, Bartholomew had been praying for the coming of the Messiah.

Read the narrative of Nathanael Bartholomew, recorded in John 1:43-51, and illustrate portions of the scripture passage by making an accordion-folded book. Depict parts of the story on separate pages of the book. Include themes like: Bartholomew sitting under the fig tree praying; Philip coming to tell him about Jesus; Bartholomew questioning Philip; Philip's invitation to "Come and see"; Going to meet Jesus; Jesus telling Bartholomew he already knew all about him; Bartholomew's proclamation that Jesus was the son of God and so forth. Also include some pages about places that you like to go to read the Bible or pray, and ways that you tell someone else about Jesus through your words and actions.

For each book, choose as many pieces of posterboard as there will be pages of the story. On each page, use markers or crayons to draw and write about the scene, or cut pictures and words from used church school papers,

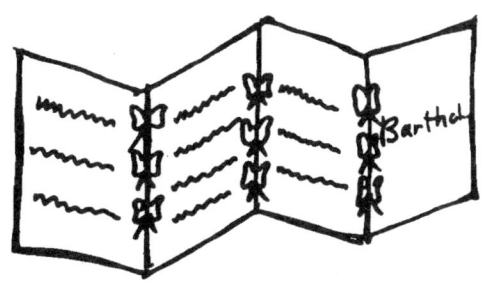

magazines and newspapers, and glue them in place. Create a cover which includes the word, "Bartholomew." Punch three holes in the sides of each page and the cover. Use yarn, string or ribbon to lace the sheets together. Fold the book accordion style. Trade books with others in the class and see how many different ways there are to illustrate the story. Use the book to retell the account of Bartholomew to younger children, family members and friends.

BARTHOLOMEW AS A WITNESS

Supplies:
- ❑ Plastic milk jugs, 1 gallon size
- ❑ Unlined index cards, 5" x 7"
- ❑ Scissors
- ❑ Colored pencils or fine-tipped markers

Advance Preparation:
- Thoroughly clean and de-label milk jugs.

Bartholomew was one of the disciples who changed from being skeptical about Jesus to one who proclaimed him to be the son of God, the king of Israel. What caused him to believe? During their first meeting, Bartholomew was amazed that Jesus already knew of his activities and whereabouts (John 1:47-50). In addition to his personal experience with Jesus, Bartholomew witnessed major events that convinced him Jesus was the son of God.

Several days after Jesus began choosing his disciples, they were all invited to a wedding in Cana of Galilee. Cana was the hometown of Bartholomew, so it is assumed he attended with the others. When the wine for the wedding celebration ran out, Jesus asked servants to fill large stone jars with water. The disciples saw that the water had become wine, and because of the miracle, they believed Jesus had revealed his glory. (John 2:1-11)

There is not much recorded about Bartholomew or his work after he became a disciple; however, he was one of the seven named in John 21:1-14 who met Jesus, the risen Lord, on the shores of the Sea of Galilee.

Both of these Bible passages bring vivid pictures to mind. Construct a simple viewer to enjoy illustrations of these exciting stories. To construct the viewer, remove the cap and any labels from an empty, clean milk jug. Using scissors, cut a slit on the side of the bottle opposite the handle, about two inches up from the bottom of the jug. The slit will have to be wide enough so the five inch end of the card will fit into the container. Place the milk jug aside.

Read the two miracle stories in the Bible, then decide how to portray the events. Place the 5" x 7" card vertically in front of you. Illustrate the stories, using the bottom 2/3rds of the cards. On the top of each card, write a title describing the action. The entire happening may appear on one card or on several cards to develop the sequence of events. If more than one card is used, be sure to add numbers at the top to keep them in order.

You may want to add captions or scripture references under the picture. When all of the work on the cards is finished, slide the cards into the slot of the milk jug viewer. Hold the viewer with the handle down and the card slot on top. Look through the neck opening to "witness" the miracles that helped Bartholomew know Jesus as the son of God.

BARTHOLOMEW AS A MISSIONARY

Supplies:

- Steel wool
- Pen or pencil
- Scraps of posterboard or wood
- Shield pattern
- Carbon paper
- Glue that will adhere to metal
- Metal foil (34 gauge copper, aluminum or brass, available at craft stores) or aluminum foil pans
- Tools for embossing (pointed dowels, popsicle sticks, plastic or wooden utensils, pencils with broken lead)
- Newspaper
- Scratch paper
- Patterns or photos of knives
- Tape
- Utility shears

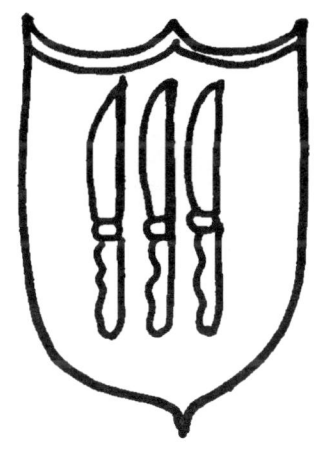

Bartholomew's skepticism changed to faithful discipleship. Tradition tells us that Nathanael Bartholomew served as a missionary in India, Ethiopia, Persia, Asia Minor and Armenia. Some historians say Bartholomew started the Christian Church in India and established the Church of Armenia.

It is reported that Bartholomew's powerful preaching convinced many Armenian people to believe in Jesus Christ instead of their pagan gods. When the king and other leaders were baptized, the pagan priests and the king's brother planned Bartholomew's death. The disciple was arrested, then he was martyred in Armenia by flaying, which means to strip off a person's skin. The traditional symbol for Bartholomew's shield pictures one knife, or a row of three knives, representing his cruel death.

Design a shield depicting Bartholomew's symbol. Discover an ancient form of art know as metal tooling or embossing. Cut metal foil into rectangles approximately 6" by 7". If using foil baking pans, choose pieces with the smoothest surface. Be careful! Cut edges will be sharp. Tape along edges to prevent injuries and to form a margin. Prepare plans on scratch paper the same size as the metal piece. Use the photos or patterns of knives to aid in sketching the symbols. Place the metal foil on a pad of newspaper. Lay the drawing on the metal piece and trace with a pencil or stick. There will be an impression of the design on the metal. Decide which parts of the symbol will be raised and which parts will be depressed. Place the foil on a soft pad of newspaper. Continue to form the design by pressing into the metal with a smooth tool until the symbols are raised. Turn the piece, first to one side, then

Disciples Then! Disciples Now! — 53

the other, pressing from both sides.

When the embossing process is complete, pull off the tape and polish the surface with steel wool. Trim the foil into the shape of a shield. Select either wood or posterboard for the base, then glue the metal tooling to the background. Display the tooled symbol as a reminder of Bartholomew, one of the faithful followers of Jesus.

Chapter Eight

Thomas

In the Gospels of Matthew, Mark and Luke, Thomas is named as one of the twelve special disciples of Jesus, but nothing further is said about him in these three books. Thomas plays an important role, however, in the book of John. Two statements recorded in John will always be associated with Thomas. The first declaration, "I am the Way and the Truth and the Life. No one comes to the Father except through me," (John 14:6) was made by Jesus to Thomas after Jesus told his faithful followers that he would be leaving; that he would be going to prepare a place for them. Thomas asked Jesus "where" he was going and the "way" the rest of the disciples could go there, too. In response Jesus made this powerful proclamation which has been used by countless numbers throughout the centuries to share the Gospel story. The second affirmation of faith was made by Thomas after he saw Jesus, the risen Lord. Since Thomas was not with the disciples at the time of Jesus' appearance, he doubted the resurrection and stated that he would have to see the nail marks for himself before he would believe this incredible story. Once Thomas saw Jesus he immediately exclaimed, "My Lord and my God!" (John 20:24-28)

Besides these "two" important testimonies associated with this disciple, the entire story of Thomas' life has the number "two" associated with it. Use the activities in this learning center to learn more of his "Two Names: Thomas and Didymus," "Two Attributes: Doubt and Belief," "Two Questions: Where? and Way?," "Two Affirmations: My Lord and my God" and "Two Occupations: Tradesman and Missionary."

THOMAS' TWO NAMES: THOMAS AND DIDYMUS

Supplies:
- Construction paper, 9" x 12"
- Scissors
- Markers
- Pencils
- Glue sticks
- Bibles

In spite of the fact that we know very little about the disciple Thomas, we do have interesting information about his name. He was known as "Thomas" in Hebrew, or "Didymus" in Greek. In either language, his name meant "twin," however, we do not know who the other person was or if he actually had a twin.

Some ancient writers speculate that Thomas or Didymus could have been surnames and that the disciple's first name was not recorded. In most versions of the Bible, this apostle is referred to as "Thomas called Didymus" or "Thomas the twin." (John 11:16 and John 21:2) "Twin" may have been used as a nickname for Thomas to imply personal traits similar to those of another believer. We may never know the true meaning of Thomas' name, but throughout the Christian world, he is called by still another title, "Doubting Thomas."

We discover a lot about the disciples when we learn about their names. Create a double name design as a reminder of the biblical references to Thomas/Didymus.

Select a piece of 9" x 12" colored paper and fold it in half length-wise. Write the selected name in cursive so that the letters rest directly on the folded edge. Letters with loops extending below the line will have to be formed with only the top portion showing. Draw the name with double pencil lines or a very thick line. Cut on both sides of the letters. Be certain that the letters are attached to each other along the fold so the name will be intact when the cutting is done. Carefully unfold the cut-out and glue to construction paper of a contrasting color.

Make several "twin" name designs to see the images formed by different combinations of letters. On the bottom of the mounted name design, write one of the scripture passages which refers to Thomas/Didymus.

THOMAS' TWO ATTRIBUTES: DOUBT AND BELIEF

Supplies:
- ❑ Bible
- ❑ Pens or pencils
- ❑ Thesaurus or book of synonyms
- ❑ Paper
- ❑ Dictionary

There are two ways to look at the life of Thomas. One is to emphasize his negative characteristics, such as disbelief and doubt. The other is to examine his positive attributes like devotion and dedication. John 11:1-44, the death and resurrection of Lazarus, is a good passage to use for exploring the positive theme.

When Mary and Martha sent word to Jesus about the illness of their brother Lazarus, Jesus delayed going to Bethany in response to their request. Later, when Jesus announced that he was going to the home of his friends, the disciples protested because they feared Jesus would be harmed or killed by those who opposed his teachings. Thomas declared that he thought the disciples should accompany Jesus to Bethany, probably to protect him. Thomas, often known as the doubter, showed his courage and conviction when he declared that if Jesus was to die, he was willing to die, too. (John 11:16)

Read the scripture account of the illness, death and resurrection of Jesus' friend, Lazarus, and pay special attention to Thomas' role in the story. Using a pencil or pen, make a list on paper of the positive characteristics of the disciple Thomas. Include words like loyal, courageous and devoted. Use a dictionary to look up the meaning of each word on the paper and write a short, simple definition next to the word. If possible, find a synonym, a word with a similar meaning, for each item on the list and write these words on the roster, too. Review the list and make a check mark next to the positive qualities of a disciple that you show or would like to show.

THOMAS' TWO QUESTIONS: WHERE? AND WAY?

Supplies:
- Plastic caps from milk jugs
- Scissors
- Scrap paper
- Markers, fine-tipped
- Craft glue
- Bible
- Awl or compass point
- Elastic cord
- Pencils
- Beads or sequins
- Darning needle

Advance Preparation:
- Wash and dry plastic milk caps.

Doubting Thomas was the disciple who searched for answers and asked for proof. He found some of the things Jesus said difficult to understand and hard to believe at first.

Jesus had just finished telling the disciples that he was leaving and that he was going to prepare a place for them in God's house. Trying to understand, Thomas asked Jesus where he was going and how would they know the way to get there too. (John 14:1-5) Jesus answered: "I am the Way, and the Truth, and the Life. No one comes to the Father except through me. If you know me, you will know my Father also. From now on you do know him and you have seen him." (John 14:6,7)

Continue reading the rest of the message Jesus gave to his followers to help them comprehend his mission. (John 14:8-14) Assemble a wrist band to help you remember the words of Jesus: WAY, TRUTH, LIFE.

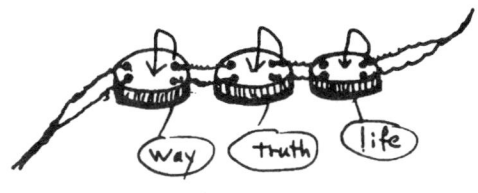

Each wrist band will require three colored milk jug caps and two pieces of elastic cord, plus paper and beads or sequins for trim. Be certain the milk jug caps are clean and dry. Cut two pieces of elastic cord about eight inches long. Choose three bottle caps, then poke four holes into each one—two on one edge and two directly opposite. With the help of a darning needle, thread the elastic pieces through the holes. The caps will be connected at the top and bottom. Tie both strips of elastic to fit your wrist and trim off any extra elastic. Be sure each lid is

Disciples Then! Disciples Now! — 57

positioned so the flat, topside is facing out. Using paper, pencil and a lid, trace three circles and cut them out. Write or print one of these words on each of the paper circles: WAY, TRUTH, LIFE. Glue the paper to the plastic caps and if you wish, decorate with tiny beads or sequins.

When you wear the wrist band, remember that if Thomas was not sure about an answer or when he was filled with doubt, he showed courage by asking questions. Use the wristband to explain the story to other people, and to be assured that Jesus is indeed the WAY, the TRUTH and the LIFE.

THOMAS' TWO AFFIRMATIONS: MY LORD AND MY GOD

Supplies:
- White construction paper
- Black tempera paint
- Shallow pan for paint
- Paper clips
- Crayons
- Paint brushes
- Scissors
- Chalk dust, talc or cleanser

Thomas was not with the other disciples when Jesus appeared to them on the day of the resurrection, therefore he doubted that their incredible story could be true. In fact, Thomas stated that he would have to "see" before he would "believe." A week later when Jesus appeared again, Thomas was convinced and immediately declared, "My Lord and my God!" (John 20:28)

It is often difficult to believe things that we cannot see. Use a special type of painting, called crayon etching, to help you remember Thomas' powerful statement of faith, "My Lord and my God!" Choose a piece of white construction paper and write Thomas' words on it. Draw symbols associated with Jesus' resurrection, like butterflies and flowers, on the page. Choose brightly colored crayons and fill in the words and symbols with solid, steady strokes. Cover the drawing with a light coating of chalk dust, talc or cleanser so the paint will adhere. Using the black tempera paint, brush the entire drawing with this liquid. Allow the picture to dry for a few minutes. Use a scissor blade or opened paper clip to gently scrape away some of the black so the colorful words and symbols show through. Display the picture in the classroom, church, school or home.

THOMAS' TWO OCCUPATIONS: TRADESMAN AND MISSIONARY

Supplies:
- Tacks or brads, 1/2"
- Sandpaper
- Pencils
- Felt
- Newspaper
- Tack hammer
- Ruler
- Markers, fine-tipped
- Glue
- Blocks of wood, about 4" x 4" x 1"
- Picture of spear, carpenter square or complete symbol for Thomas

The apostle Thomas appears in scripture with some of the disciples who were fishermen. Maybe as a young man he fished with the others, but history tells us he was a builder. In some accounts, he is described as a stonemason, but most records state he was a carpenter.

Thomas can also be considered a "builder" in his second important occupation—missionary. It is recorded that he traveled to India to spread the teachings of Jesus. Christians in India often called themselves "Christians of Saint Thomas." Thomas, the missionary, had many opportunities to use his skills as a tradesman and his faith as a disciple to build churches for God's kingdom.

The traditional symbol for Thomas is a carpenter's square, representing the way he worked, and a vertical spear, denoting the way he died. It is written that he was martyred in India and that he was buried in Mylapore, near Madras. It is believed that when pagan religious leaders became envious of his ministry, they encouraged the people to stone Thomas, and finally kill him with a spear.

You will create a symbol incorporating important aspects of his life. The finished project can be used as a paperweight.

Cover the work surface with newspaper and sand the wood block until it is smooth all over. Draw an oval or shield shape nearly as large as the wood block. Carefully pound the tacks into the wood, following the marked outline.

Inside the nail border, use a pencil and ruler to draw the carpenter's right angle tool and the spear. Trace over the pencil lines with marking pens to emphasize the implements.

Turn the paperweight bottom side up and glue a square of felt to the wood block. Place the finished piece somewhere to help you think about the Thomas who doubted at first, but then became a loyal believer and missionary, or "builder of churches."

Chapter Nine

Matthew

Matthew is listed in the Gospels of Matthew, Mark and Luke as one of the twelve disciples. According to the book of Matthew, he was a tax collector who was sitting in his toll booth when Jesus passed by and called him to "Follow" (Matthew 9:9). Later this Gospel lists the same man as one of the disciples (10:3). Mark and Luke also include the story of the tax collector, but they name him Levi and do not identify him with the disciple Matthew. Because of his profession, Matthew was probably the most well-educated, the wealthiest and the most sophisticated of the Twelve. Using these gifts in the service of the savior, Matthew's life changed from being a tax collector to becoming a disciple, a host, a missionary and a writer. By participating in the five activities in this learning center, participants will meet Matthew the Tax Collector, and learn that Jesus can use everyone's skills and abilities for his service; Matthew the Host, and realize that Jesus came to love all types of people; Matthew the Disciple, and discover more about the person and work of Christ; Matthew the Missionary, and be reminded to spread God's love to everyone; and Matthew the Writer, and observe that the book of Matthew identifies Jesus as the fulfillment of God's promises to the Hebrew people. To emphasize the changes that took place in Matthew's life, the materials for each learning activity are those which "change" in form or function from the beginning to the end of the project.

MATTHEW ----THE TAX COLLECTOR

Supplies:
- ❑ Naugahyde or leather-looking fabric, such as suede cloth
- ❑ Circle patterns, 8" diameter and 6" diameter
- ❑ Rotary punch for leather or paper punch
- ❑ Dressmaker's chalk or marker   ❑ Cord
- ❑ Ruler   ❑ Scissors

Matthew was an unlikely person for Jesus to select as a disciple. He was a tax collector, or publican, which was one of the most despised occupations of Jesus' time. Matthew gathered tolls near Capernaum and perhaps assessed industries such as fishing.

The Romans had taken over the land of Israel and wanted tax money for their own support. In some cases, Jewish citizens worked for the Roman leaders and collected money from fellow Jews. The Roman government determined a certain amount for taxes, allowing the publicans to keep any surplus for their own salary. Many tax collectors became wealthy because they overcharged the people in their districts.

We learn a lot about Matthew when we see that Jesus asked him to leave everything behind and follow him. Matthew seemed to respond without any questions or hesitation. Why would Jesus ask someone with such an undesirable occupation to accompany him? Jesus can use anyone to spread the story of his love.

Symbols traditionally associated with Matthew are money pouches. In this activity, consider the pouch a symbol of the positive influence of Matthew, instead of a reminder of his dreaded occupation. Use the pouch as a "bank" to save a portion of earned money or to gather loose change.

To make a bank, trace the 8" pattern onto the fabric or Naugahyde and cut out the circle. Center the 6" pattern on the cloth circle and mark a dot approximately every inch around the outside edge of the pattern. Punch a hole wherever a dot is marked.

To form a drawstring pouch, cut two pieces of cord about 16" long. Thread one end of the cord through all the holes until it reaches the starting place. Tie together the two ends of the first cord. Begin threading the second piece through the holes directly opposite the first set; then tie those ends together. Grasp the two sets of knotted ends and pull them in opposite directions to close the drawstring pouch.

Plan on your own or with the class to donate the money collected for a special mission project or other needed cause. The pouch can remind you of one of the changes in Matthew's life ... from a disliked tax collector to a valued disciple.

MATTHEW----THE HOST

Supplies:
- Construction paper, 12" x 18"
- Rulers
- Pencils
- Glue
- Scrap paper
- Clear adhesive backed paper
- Scissors
- Small heart patterns
- Crayons or markers
- Bible
- Materials for chosen method of creating the border

To everyone's surprise, including Matthew himself, Jesus called the tax collector to be one of his disciples. Possibly, as a way to introduce his new Master or to show his appreciation for being chosen, Matthew hosted a grand banquet. Jesus was invited, as well as many tax collectors. Matthew wanted everyone to understand that Jesus was the Messiah for all people, even the despised publicans. The new disciple learned firsthand that Jesus looked into people's hearts and considered their true character, even if they were social outcasts.

The Scribes and Pharisees seemed shocked that Jesus would associate with such undesirable people. When they asked the disciples for an explanation,

Jesus answered: "Those who are well have no need of a physician, but those who are sick; I have come to call not the righteous but sinners (Mark 2:17; Luke 5:31-2). Matthew was a living sign that all sinners are welcome in our Lord's kingdom.

Design a placemat to indicate the importance of this special event. Decorate with a heart motif as a reminder that Jesus judges us by what is in our heart, not by our appearance.

Choose a sheet of construction paper for the placemat. Create a border design with a combination of materials such as a heart and a paper punch, heart stickers or heart-shaped rubber stamps. Add Matthew's name or verses of scripture with neatly written letters and be certain to glue any cut-out or punched-out hearts in place.

Measure a piece of clear adhesive-backed paper larger than the decorated construction paper mat. Carefully peel off the paper backing and begin to position the covering over the top surface of the placemat. Be sure that some of the clear paper extends beyond the construction paper. In order to protect the designed portions and all the edges of the mat, fold the surplus covering to the back.

Plan to "host" your own party. It would be fun to have each guest create his or her own placemat as part of the activities. Use the mat made in the learning center for an example.

MATTHEW----THE DISCIPLE

Supplies:
- ❑ Bible
- ❑ Posterboard
- ❑ Markers
- ❑ Parallel Bible
- ❑ Scissors
- ❑ Pipe cleaners

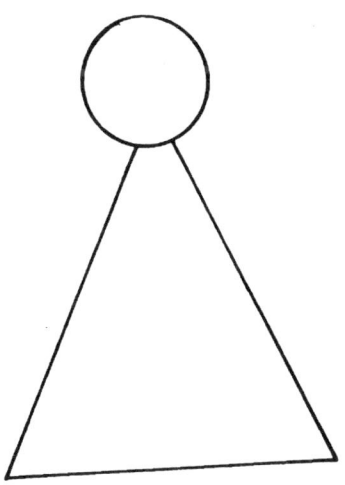

Matthew was an eyewitness to the fact that God fulfilled his promises to the Hebrew people by sending Jesus to be the redeemer of the world. Matthew's Gospel records several stories and events that took place during Jesus' ministry that are not found in the books of Mark, Luke and John. Some of these are the visit of the Magi (2:1-12), the escape to Egypt (2:13-15), Jesus healing two blind men (9:27-31) and the Parable of the Unforgiving Servant (18:23-35).

Illustrate one or more of Matthew's special accounts by making and using finger puppets to tell the story. Begin by choosing a passage, only found in the book of Matthew, to portray. If possible, look in a Parallel Bible to determine some of the stories that are only contained in the first Gospel. For each person in the story, cut a 3" triangle from posterboard to serve as the body and a 1/2" circle from posterboard for the head.

Near the base of the triangle, cut two circles. Two of your fingers will go through these holes and become the puppet's legs. To create

Disciples Then! Disciples Now! — 63

arms, glue a pipe cleaner on the back of the puppet, below the top point of the triangle. Glue the circle, or head, to the top of the triangle. Using a marker, draw a face on the head and any desired details on the costume. Complete the puppet by placing your first two fingers through the holes to form the legs. Make and use as many puppets as needed to present the Bible story.

MATTHEW----THE MISSIONARY

Supplies:
- T-shirts
- Paper
- Iron
- Brown paper
- Fabric crayons
- Pencils
- Ironing board

Advance Preparation:
- Ask each student to bring a t-shirt.
- Arrange for adult supervision at the ironing station.
- Prepare sheets with t-shirt washing instructions, as indicated on the fabric crayon box.

After the ascension, Matthew is believed to have preached in Africa. The most popular tradition is that he carried the Gospel to Ethiopia. It is not known for sure how he died, but it is thought that he was martyred for the sake of the Gospel. Although we do not have much information about Matthew's mission, we do know about his message. Matthew was a witness to the fact that Jesus came to be the Savior of all people, even the most unlikely.

Jesus entrusted the disciples with the task of spreading the message of God's love. He told them to preach and teach and baptize in his name. This message was spread with words and actions, as well as non-verbally. Today people often wear clothing that contains words or symbols which communicate powerful Christian messages. Make a t-shirt with words and/or symbols to help communicate Jesus' love.

Create the design on a piece of paper. If words are used, be sure all the letters are written in reverse. Use fabric crayons and color the designs. Color with solid, steady strokes and outline the letters in black so they stand out in the design.

64 — Disciples Then! Disciples Now!

Ask an adult to help with the rest of the process. Bring your t-shirt and drawing to the ironing station. Position the front of the shirt over the board and center the paper with coloring face-down on it. Cover the design with brown paper. Iron the design into the fabric, using a firm, steady downward pressing motion. Do not slide the iron back and forth. The iron must be very hot for the design to transfer properly. Carefully remove the papers from the shirt. Before leaving the learning center, take home a sheet of washing instructions.

Wear the shirt and remember that just as Matthew was a missionary in his day, you are a missionary in your present situation.

MATTHEW----THE WRITER

Supplies:
- Absorbent paper such as newsprint or tissue
- Food coloring or cold-water, non-toxic dyes
- Protective covering for artists and work surface
- Drying space or clothesline and clip clothespins
- Heavy cardboard, such as tablet backs or thick posterboard
- White or light colored construction paper, 12" x 18"
- Rulers
- Scissors
- Pencils
- Glue
- Clean-up supplies
- Markers
- Bible
- Ribbon

Advance Preparation:
- Pour dye into containers.
- Determine space for drying.
- Cut cardboard into 6" squares, two for each book.
- Cut the 12" x 18" paper into 6" x 18" strips, allowing one or two pieces for each book.

Matthew was an educated man who was accustomed to keeping records as a tax collector. It appears that he applied the same organizational skills to the writing of the Gospel attributed to him.

All of the Gospel writers included most of the important information about Jesus, but there were some differences. In addition to the general information about the life and teachings of Jesus, Matthew included his childhood as well as a more detailed account of the resurrection. Matthew especially emphasized that Jesus is the Messiah mentioned in the prophecies of the Old Testament. Sometimes the book of Matthew is called the "Gospel of the Kingdom" because he refers to the "kingdom of heaven" more than fifty times. It appears that his writings were directed to the Jewish community.

Instead of recording the events in the order in which they took place, Matthew grouped Jesus' teachings in this way: the Sermon on the Mount (Matthew 5-7); the Instructions to the Disciples (Chapter 10); a Collection of Parables (Chapter 13); Relationships within the Church (Chapter 18); and the Discourse on the End of the World (Chapters 24-25). Many people believe that these five themes form a new Torah, the name given to the first five books of the Bible, for God's people. It was a useful guide for the early Church and is a means of instruction for Christians today, as well.

Look through the book of Matthew and note some passages you have heard in church school. You may choose to write some of the familiar scriptures in the book you will be making.

To create the book cover, fold the absorbent paper into fourths length-wise, then fold that narrow piece into fourths to form a small bundle. Rub scissor blades or the ruler along the edges of the folded bundle to make sharp creases. The pattern is formed by dipping corners in different colors of dye until all four corners are dyed. Mix colors by dipping a corner into more than one color or by allowing the paper to stay in the solution a little longer. Carefully unfold the wet paper and let it dry by smoothing it out on a flat surface or by hanging it on a clothesline. Be sure to have enough decorated paper for the front and back book covers.

While the "fold and dye" piece is drying, form the pages of the book. Accordion-fold or fan-fold one or two strips of 6" by 18" paper into 6" squares. If two strips are joined, overlap two of the sections and glue neatly to form a 6" by 30" piece.

When the dyed piece is dry, make the book cover by wrapping it around the 6" cardboard square. Position the paper to display the most attractive portion of the design. Allow enough paper to fold about 2" around to the back of the cardboard. Trim off any excess and be sure to smooth before gluing. Continue by gluing one end of the accordion-folded pages to the back side of the cardboard, covering the flipped over edges. Repeat the same process for the other covered cardboard and the other end of the folded pages. Put heavy books or magazines on the finished book as the glue dries. Tie a ribbon around the accordion-folded book for a decorative touch and to help the pages stay closed.

Now the book is ready for you to enter some meaningful passages from the writings of Matthew, or you may choose to use it as a journal to record your own thoughts. This handmade book will be a perfect place to gather treasured writings ... either yours or another author's work. Consider making another book to give away!

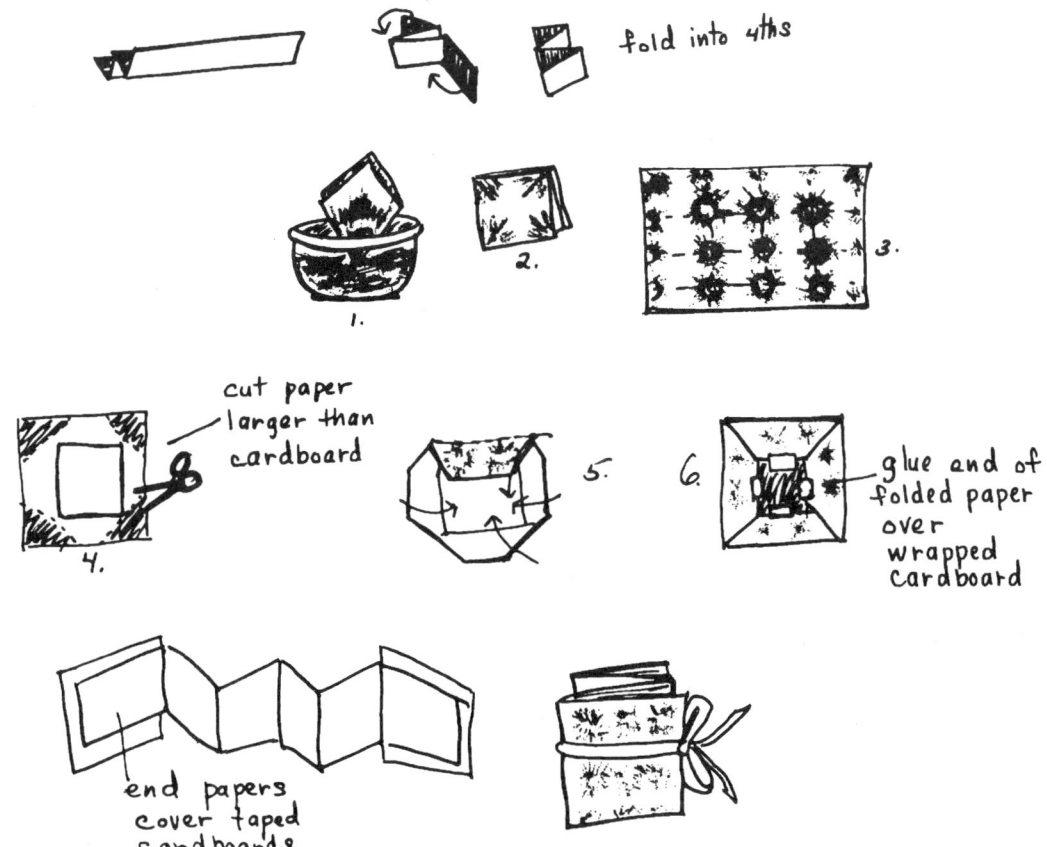

Chapter Ten

James The Less

James was a popular name among Jews because Jacob, its Hebrew form, was the name of the beloved Old Testament patriarch. Besides James, called the Less, or the son of Alphaeus, there was the disciple James, the Greater, or the son of Zebedee, who was the brother of another disciple, John. Sometimes James the Less is also confused with James the brother of the Lord, but it seems that Jesus' sibling was not a believer and a follower until after the resurrection (John 7:5; I Corinthians 15:7). Still another James associated with Jesus' friends was the father of Judas, who was not Judas Iscariot (Luke 6:16). Although confusion exists about the identity of James the Less, the mention of his name in the list of those whom the Lord chose makes him important.

Although many people consider the identity of James the Less to be a mystery, there are important lessons to learn from his life. A clue to unravel the mystery is provided in each of the learning center activities. Each four letter word—less, Mary, life, nine and sign—is the basis for an activity designed to help participants learn more about the various aspects of the life of James the Less, a disciple of Jesus.

JAMES: LESS

Supplies:
- Writing paper
- Lemon juice
- Lamp
- Toothpick or skewer
- Small jar for juice

There are many unanswered questions about the disciple called James the Less or James the son of Alphaeus. It is believed that his title, "the Less," refers to his younger age or his shorter stature. He may have been given a descriptive name to help distinguish him from the other disciple named James the son of Zebedee, also called James the Greater. In most cases, people in Bible times did not use last names; they were described by family connections or personal characteristics.

When we hear the words "less" or "greater," we may think the titles relate to the person's significance. The labels were probably given to the disciples by their peers. We may not have any information telling us why James the son of Alpheus was called to follow Jesus, but the fact that he was one of the Twelve explains his importance.

Size, age, name and shape do not matter when Jesus calls us to follow him. Why would Jesus choose you? Sometimes Jesus saw potential in a person that others missed. Think about some of your qualities which Jesus would notice. Spend a little time reflecting on your qualities or special traits. Is there something about you that other people miss, but that Jesus would notice?

Dip the wooden writing tool in the lemon juice, then write your thoughts on paper. When the lemon juice is dry, hold the paper near a heat source like a lamp. The heat causes the lemon juice to scorch, making the hidden words appear. Be careful with the lamp. The writing was there all along, but warmth and light were necessary to make it visible. In the same way, we may have hidden characteristics that become visible when someone recognizes our potential. Even though most of the life of James the Less is invisible to us, Jesus saw how he could be valuable as a follower.

JAMES: MARY

Supplies:
- Paper
- Construction paper
- Scissors
- Empty, de-labeled cans
- Paper clips
- Pencils or pens
- Markers
- Branches
- Rocks

Very little information is recorded about the disciple known as James the Less, or James the Little. Apparently, his name had "the Little" or "the Less" tacked on to distinguish him from the other James who was taller and bigger, and possibly older. Big James was John's brother and the son of Zebedee. Little James was probably the son of Alphaeus. That might have made Matthew and James brothers. If that is true, James could have been a tax collector before he became a disciple.

Of one thing we can be sure. James' mother's name was Mary, and she was one of the women who was devoted to Jesus. Mary stood at the foot of the cross at Jesus' crucifixion and visited the sepulcher early Easter morning. Some people speculate that Mary, the mother of James the Less, might have been a sister of Mary the mother of Jesus, and others think that Alphaeus may have been a brother of Joseph. Although the data for James' family tree is uncertain, we can assume that his parents had a strong influence on his faith development.

Think about your family of faith and make a "family tree" to illustrate the people who have had a role in helping you learn about Jesus' love. Use a piece of paper and a pen or pencil and make a list of several of these folks. Include parents, family members, friends, teachers, pastors, camp counselors and others who, through word and action, have influenced your faith development. Select different colors of construction paper and markers and make a "leaf" or symbol associated with each of the people on your list. Write the name of each person on a separate piece of paper and add additional words or drawings to describe the way in which the individual has helped you learn about Jesus. Cut each shape to a size that will fit on a tree branch. Choose a small branch and place it in the center of a can. Anchor the branch by filling the can with rocks. Poke a hole through each paper symbol, hook an opened paper clip through it and attach the papers to the branch. Display the "family of faith tree" in a place where you will be reminded of the important contribution of each person.

JAMES: LIFE

Supplies:

- Socks, two per person
- Scissors
- Buttons
- Brushes
- Needles
- Cardboard
- Ribbons and trims
- Fabric paints
- Permanent marking pens
- Thread

There are many ways to let other people know that you love Jesus. James the Less, like many Christians throughout history, served the Lord in quiet and unassuming ways. In fact, the Bible does not record one deed done or one word spoken by James, and yet he was a person who played an important role in Jesus' mission and ministry. We know that he responded to the call, that he went out with the Twelve, that he remained in the service of the Lord all the way through the crucifixion, death, resurrection and ascension, and that he was present in Jerusalem after the ascension. We can assume that James ministered efficiently and effectively, although what he did never made the "headlines."

Think of people you know who minister in many ways, yet their names never appear in the church bulletin or the congregational newsletter. Some people pray for missionaries on a daily basis, others bring food to someone in need, and many visit the sick and the shut-ins. Think about ways in which you show others that you love Jesus. In addition to the words you speak, there are many non-verbal ways in which this message is communicated. One is by the clothes that you wear. Turn something as simple as a pair of socks into a "statement" that you are a disciple of Jesus.

Select a pair of socks. Write these words on a piece of paper: "I could use this sock to ..." Write a list of uses such as: wear on my foot, make a puppet, wash a window, wipe a tear or dust a table. Now think of ways in which something as simple as a sock could be used to share your love for Jesus. Using the same phrase, write additional ideas such as: contribute it to a care basket, protect my feet during a hunger walk or start a fundraising project. Now, decorate the socks with words and symbols that will "tell" people who see them that you are a follower of Jesus. First, think of messages that can be placed on the socks, such as "Jesus loves me," "Say no to drugs," or "I'm special!" Also think about symbols that can be drawn on or attached to the socks. These include hearts to signify love, a cross to represent commitment to Christ and flowers or leaves to symbolize growing as a follower of Jesus.

Before beginning to decorate the socks, designate a left one and a right one. Choose from the decorating materials. To attach ribbons and three dimensional objects such as buttons to the socks, fold down the sock cuffs. Cut ribbon to the desired lengths and tie the pieces into bows. Using a threaded needle, tack a bow on each cuff, sewing through the top layer only. If using paint or markers, cut strips of cardboard and place them inside the socks to absorb excess paint. Draw or write slogans and symbols on the socks.

Disciples Then! Disciples Now!

Once the socks are completed, wear them as a visible symbol that you are a disciple of Jesus.

JAMES: NINE

Supplies:
- Bible
- Paper strips, 1" x 2"
- Tape
- Pencil
- Jumbo paper clips
- Scissors

Although the Bible, as well as historical accounts, gives very little information or background on James the Less, we know that he was important enough to be chosen as a disciple and that he was present at several major events in Jesus' life. In fact, James, the son of Alphaeus, is listed ninth in all four rosters of the Twelve: Matthew 10:3, Mark 3:18, Luke 6:15, and Acts 1:13. Some of the links we have connecting James with Jesus and his ministry are nine scripture passages. What can you learn about James the Less by reading the following passages? Look up these verses in the Bible: Matthew 10:3, Matthew 27:56, Mark 2:14, Mark 3:18, Mark 15:40, Mark 16:1, Luke 6:15, Luke 24:10 and Acts 1:13.

Link the information together by making a unique chain of paper clips. Count out nine large paper clips. Cut paper into nine small strips, 1" x 2". One or more colors of paper may be used for the project. Copy one scripture reference on each of the paper strips until all of the verses are written. Use a small bit of tape to anchor one end of a strip to the center of a clip. Roll the paper around the clip until it is all rolled up. Tuck the loose end under one of the parts of the clip; fasten with a tiny piece of tape if necessary. On the blank side of each paper wrapped clip, write a word or draw a picture that will help you remember the information about James contained in that particular verse. Attach the second clip and repeat the process. Continue until all nine clips are used.

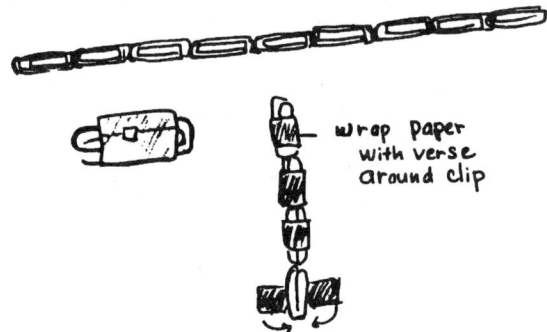
wrap paper with verse around clip

This short chain is a symbol of some of the information we know about James. Use the chain as a bookmark or hang it in your room as a reminder of what you have learned about James. Every link represents James' connection with Jesus. What are your "links" to Jesus?

JAMES: SIGN

Supplies:

- Paper
- Self-stick labels, 2" x 3"
- Carbon paper, ink stamp pad and assorted rubber stamps
- Pencils
- Permanent markers with fine points

All of the disciples have a designated symbol. Some represent the person's life and many depict the way he died. The symbol for James the Less is a saw, but there are conflicting reports about his death. Some historical accounts and many paintings show his symbol as a club. Most likely he was a martyr, that is, put to death for what he believed about Jesus.

A symbol is something that represents something else: a cross for Christianity, a plus sign (+) for addition, a dollar sign ($) for money. Sometimes a symbol stands for an abstract idea, such as a lion for courage or an oak tree for strength. Symbols are visible in every aspect of our lives: church, school, sports, food, advertisements, weather, safety and more.

Prepare a sheet of paper with several general headings across the top such as: MODERN DAY, BIBLICAL, PERSONAL. Under each heading, list symbols that come to mind. You may include the golden arches for McDonalds, a dove for the Holy Spirit or a drawing of the type of ball used in your favorite sport. See how many symbols you can recall in five minutes. Stop when you have a full page or when you run out of time.

For this activity, select one or two of the symbols which best describe you. You will make a sheet of labels which can be used on books, tapes, CD's, school supplies or any other personal belongings.

Redraw your symbol in a very simple outline form. Place the carbon paper over the sheet of blank labels and copy your symbol onto each one. Trace over the carbon line with permanent marker for a more lasting drawing. Add color accents with permanent markers.

Another method for designing personal labels would be to choose a symbol from ready-made rubber stamps. Maybe there is an animal, flower or other emblem that has special meaning for you. If the rubber stamps are printed with permanent ink, the image on the label will last much longer.

You may wish to add your name to the identification labels. If you continue to use the same symbol for a long time, people will begin to recognize who it stands for even when your name is not included.

Chapter Eleven

Jude/Thaddaeus

Although several of the disciples are known by more than one name, one of the twelve is identified by four "labels" as well as a descriptive phrase. Jude, Judas not Iscariot, Thaddaeus and Lebbaeus are words associated with a disciple about whom little is known. One question Jude asked Jesus, as well as the book of Jude which he probably wrote, gives us insight into his character, compassion, concern, convictions and commitment. Five learning center activities addressing these themes are provided. Use them to discover new insights into the life of one of Jesus' chosen followers and to detect ways of being a disciple today.

INSIGHT INTO CHARACTER

Supplies:
- Construction paper, 5" x 10"
- Scissors
- Pen
- Washable ink stamp pads
- Markers
- Wet paper towels

The disciple called Jude is sometimes referred to as Judas, not Iscariot, to show he is not the same Judas as the man who betrayed Jesus. Ironically, there is a great deal written in the scriptures about Judas Iscariot, but only one recorded event involving Jude/Thaddaeus. After the Last Supper, he asked Jesus a question, which is stated in John 14:22.

With Jude's single query we gain insight into his character. He trusted the Master enough to question him and wanted to share this "good news" with people everywhere. In spite of the confusion over names, it is clear that this Jude was a faithful follower. It is easy to separate the men named Judas when we learn how each lived his life.

Show that you are learning to be a faithful follower by displaying a doorknob hanger. Include the scripture passage: "How beautiful are the feet of those who bring good news!" (Romans 10:15)

Choose a piece of 5" x 10" paper and near the top cut slits in the shape of a plus sign (+). Place it over a doorknob to see if the opening is large enough to fit without tearing the paper. You may want to round off the top corners of the doorknob hanger or change its shape in some other way.

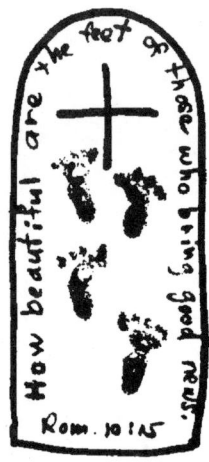

Make mini-footprints by firmly pressing the side of your curled fist onto the ink pad and then onto the paper. Along the top of the fist-print, add five "toes" by repeating the process with your index finger tip. Alternate hands to give the appearance of feet walking. There will be enough room for about three or four "beautiful feet." Use contrasting colors of paper and ink for the best results. Clean hands with wet paper towels and allow the ink prints to dry.

Neatly print or write the passage from Romans 10:15 on the paper. Display the doorknob hanger on the door to your room. As you grow in discipleship, consider this as a reminder to learn about Jesus and to show others by the way you live your life.

INSIGHT INTO COMPASSION

Supplies:

- ❑ Scissors
- ❑ Glue
- ❑ Pen
- ❑ Construction paper, two colors

Besides the names Jude, Judas and Thaddaeus, still another name, "Lebbaeus," gives us insight into the compassionate side of this follower of Jesus. Lebbaeus, the name listed in Matthew 10:3 in some manuscripts, is taken from the Hebrew word <u>leb</u>, which means "heart." Perhaps Jude was identified by his family and friends as a tender-hearted person. His whole-hearted concern for others is evident from the question he asked Jesus at the Last Supper. Regardless of the reason for the name, make a woven heart as a way to remember this important aspect of Jude/Thaddaeus' personality. Cut each color of construction paper to a 3" x 8" rectangle and fold each piece in half. Use a pencil to draw a dotted line one inch from the unfolded end of each rectangle. Hold both pieces together and cut a rounded arch on the open end above this line. Be sure both pieces are the same size. Beginning at the fold, cut two slits one inch from each side of the paper. Cut up to the dotted line on each slit. The paper will be divided into three equal strips. Write information about Jude/Thaddaeus on each of the strips. Weave the strips of paper through each other to form a heart shape. Carefully open the heart and smooth out the weaving.

Cut a 1/2" x 5" strip of construction paper to use for the handle of the woven heart. Attach the handle to the top of the heart.

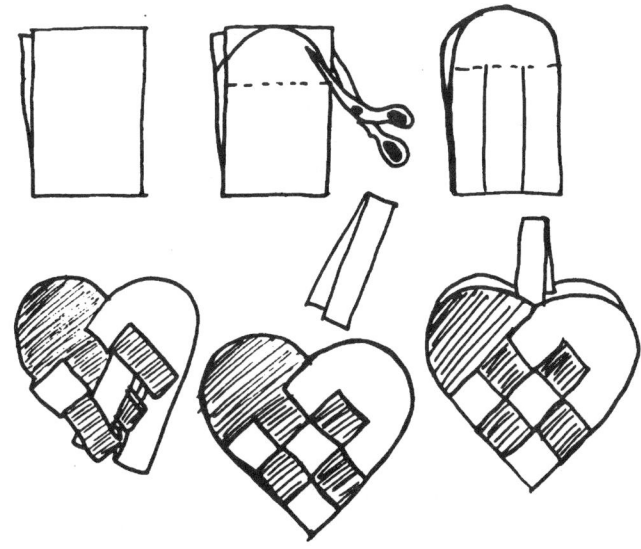

INSIGHT INTO CONCERN

Supplies:

- Circle pattern
- Scissors
- Sponges
- Thread
- Paper scraps
- Bible
- Pencil
- Green tempera paint
- Darning needle
- Newspaper
- Pen
- Blue posterboard or heavy construction paper

Jude is one of the disciples who is mentioned just a few times in the Bible. We know nothing for certain about his family or his work, but we get a glimpse of what Jude was like by a question he asked Jesus.

After the Last Supper, Jesus began instructing the disciples how to carry on without him. As he tried to comfort the Twelve, Jesus explained that he would reveal himself to those who loved him and followed his commandments. It was then that Jude asked the question, "Lord, how is it that you will reveal yourself to us, and not to the world?" (John 14:22) Read the answer that Jesus gave to Jude in John 14:23,24.

Jude was concerned about the world beyond his community. After Jesus died, Jude, as well as the other disciples, traveled to many places in the world to share the teachings of the master. The disciple's great insight was evident from his simple question. Form a mobile to symbolize Jude's regard for the world.

Place the circle pattern on the blue paper; then, trace and cut two matching circles. Cut a slit from the outer edge of the circle to the center of both pieces. Lay the circles flat on top of the newspaper-covered work surface. To give the

Disciples Then! Disciples Now! — 77

appearance of continents, tap green paint at random around both sides of the blue circles. When the paint is dry, assemble the "world," by interlocking the slit portions of the circles.

Fold a small square of red paper and cut a heart shape. Unfold the heart, and with a pen, write Jude's quotations on one side and Jesus' promise on the other. Attach the heart to the underside of the "world" using the darning needle to sew the thread through the paper. Extend the thread for several inches and then tie the ends to hold the heart in place. Provide a hanging loop for the mobile by following the same procedure with the darning needle and thread.

Hang the mobile where it can swing freely and remember Jude's concern that people everywhere learn of Jesus.

INSIGHT INTO CONVICTIONS

Supplies:
- Bible
- Pencil
- Key chain
- Acrylic paints
- Water and clean-up supplies
- Paper
- Wooden cross with pre-drilled hole
- Sandpaper
- Brushes
- Permanent markers, fine-tipped

The disciple Jude, also known as Judas or Thaddaeus, has very little written about him. We know he was special in order to have been chosen by Jesus. Some historians record that Jude preached in the Near East. Because of his strong convictions, he was able to convert many people to Christianity.

There were three men named Judas in the New Testament, but some authorities believe that this disciple is the writer of the epistle of Jude. In this book, Jude warns of false teachings and immoral living. He reminds the faithful that they must pray and rely on the power of the Holy Spirit to guide them.

Design a cross-shaped key chain as a sign of your Christian convictions. Add a meaningful prayer to help guide you along the right path.

Read the benediction at the end of the Letter of Jude, verses 24 and 25. Make up your own prayer or copy something from scripture that is helpful to you. One of these selections may be meaningful:

- "Lead me not into temptation" (Matthew 6:13)
- "By his light I walked through darkness" (Job 29:3)
- "The Lord will guide you continually" (Isaiah 58:11)
- "Teach me your way, O Lord" (Psalm 27:11)

Choose or create a prayer suitable for the key chain.

Lightly sand the wooden cross, then brush off any dusty residue. Carefully paint the cross with a color you like. Allow one side to dry before painting the other. With a tiny brush or fine-tipped permanent marker, write the short verse you have chosen. Add decorative touches. Clean up your work space. When the lettering is dry, fasten the key chain through the hole in the wooden cross. Your prayer key chain can serve as a sign of your beliefs and a reminder of the Holy Spirit's power to guide us. Think about Jude sharing his faith and instructing others how to live.

INSIGHT INTO COMMITMENT

Supplies:
- ❏ Tray
- ❏ Items related to mission profession
- ❏ Cloth
- ❏ Pens or pencils
- ❏ Paper
- ❏ Clock or watch with a second hand or digital read-out

Advance Preparation:
- Place items associated with mission professions on a tray. Include objects such as a toy airplane for a pilot, a hammer for a carpenter, seeds for an agriculturist, a cookbook for a dietitian and a Bible for a pastor. Cover the tray with a cloth.

There are traditions that Jude/Thaddaeus preached the Gospel in Judea, Samaria and Mesopotamia, and that he was martyred in Persia with his fellow apostle Simon the Zealot. Because of the many legends about Jude's missionary activity, all we can say with certainty is that he was faithful to the commission given to the Twelve, even to the point of death.

Jude's symbol in art is a sailboat, representing him as a great traveler in his missionary work for Christ. Modern day missionaries have many "symbols" associated with them, too. In this activity you are being asked to spend one minute looking at a tray of items and to remember and write down as many of them as possible. Each item on the tray can be associated with a way in which someone spreads the gospel. For example, pilots need airplanes; carpenters use saws; dietitians have cookbooks. Next to each word on your list, write a type of missionary who would use that item. After selecting a piece of paper and a pencil

Disciples Then! Disciples Now! — 79

or pen, uncover the tray. Time yourself for one minute as you view the items and try to remember as many of them as possible. Cover the tray and use the next minute to write down as many objects as you can. Now, write a mission-related profession next to each word on your list. Look at the objects on the tray again and attempt to come up with a profession associated with each item.

Chapter Twelve

Simon The Zealot

Most likely, Jesus' disciple Simon "the Zealot" had this descriptive phrase added to his name to distinguish him from Simon Peter, Andrew's brother, and from one of the brothers of Jesus who was also called Simon (Mark 6:3). Actually, Simon was the name of nine persons in the New Testament, including Simon the Pharisee (Luke 7:36-50), Simon the leper (Mark 14:3-9) and Simon of Cyrene (Matthew 27:32; Mark 15:21; Luke 23:26). Beyond identifying Simon as a Zealot, little is know about this man. Since information about the Zealot movement is recorded in history, we can surmise the type of person Simon might have been. Simon the Zealot's life exemplifies some of the qualities needed by a disciple, then and now. Activities in these five learning centers will help the participants discover the qualities Simon the Zealot demonstrated in his life: zeal, dedication, leadership, cooperation and individuality, and will suggest ways in which these same characteristics need to be displayed by Jesus' followers today.

ZEAL

Supplies:
- Pencils
- Markers
- Large drinking straws
- Ruler
- Thesaurus
- Construction paper, many colors
- Scissors
- Tape
- Dictionary
- Scrap paper

In the accounts of the twelve disciples we learn very little about Simon. The writings of Matthew and Mark refer to him as Simon the Cananaean, an Aramaic word that means "zealous." In the books of Luke and Acts he is called Simon Zelotes or Simon the Zealot. Historical information points to his association with a radical Jewish party called the Zealots. The Zealots were constantly revolting against the Roman rule. This group of fighters wanted to force the Roman conquerors out of the country.

Definitions for the word "zeal" include eager desire or effort, enthusiastic devotion and ardor, especially for a cause. It may have been Simon's desire and effort that attracted Jesus to choose him as a disciple. Enthusiasm is an important quality for a follower of Jesus. With his teachings, Jesus was able to change Simon's "zeal" for war to efforts for peace.

One way to show excitement or support is to display a pennant identifying

Disciples Then! Disciples Now! — 81

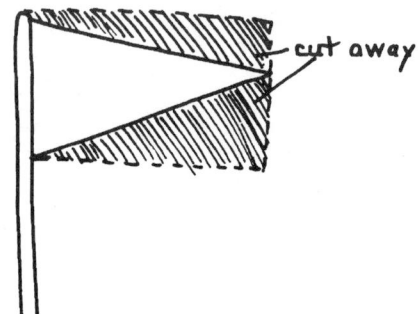

a group or cause. Design a pennant which highlights the "zeal" of Simon. Choose a piece of 9" x 12" colored paper. With a ruler and pencil, measure along one 9" side and mark the center point at 4 1/2". To form a triangular pennant shape, draw lines from the center mark on one end of the paper to both corners along the opposite edge. Cut out the triangle and set it aside.

Check meanings and synonyms for the words "zeal," "zealous" and "zealot." Write down the definitions on the scrap paper. Compose a short poem highlighting the quality of zeal as it was shown in Simon or as it is shown in you. Write the finished poem around the edges of the pennant. Tape the pennant to a straw or attach it to a bulletin board. Share your excitement about Jesus and his teachings with other people. Show your zeal!

DEDICATION

Supplies:

- ❑ Construction paper
- ❑ Glue
- ❑ Pencils
- ❑ Bibles
- ❑ Scissors
- ❑ Ruler
- ❑ Markers
- ❑ Books on historical and modern day people of faith

Simon the Zealot was a dedicated person. When Jesus called him to be a disciple, he was dedicated to the cause of overthrowing the kingdom of the Romans who were ruling Israel. During Simon's time with Jesus, he became dedicated to establishing the kingdom of God. Besides Simon the Zealot, there are numerous examples of people in the Bible, in history and in everyday life who display dedication and devotion to the cause of Christ. Learn more about them and make a string of paper figures to help you remember their stories.

Using the Bible, read the information about Simon the Zealot recorded in Luke 6:15. Look through the scripture for stories of other men and women of faith who were "zealous" for God. For example, review the accounts of the prophets in the Old Testament and the narratives about Saul/Paul in the New Testament, especially Ephesians 6:14-17. Continue learning about people of faith by looking through the resource materials available in the learning center or by recalling stories of people who demonstrate dedication to Jesus. Examples are numerous.

Fold a piece of paper, 12" or longer, into four or more equal sections. Use a ruler to measure the sections. On the top section draw a design, the shape of a person, that touches the folds on both sides in at least one place. Cut out the design but be careful not to cut away the fold at those places where it touches the edges. Glue the string of people onto another color of paper. Use markers to add details

82 — Disciples Then! Disciples Now!

and decorations. Write the name "Simon the Zealot" on the first figure, and record additional names of people of faith on the other shapes.

LEADERSHIP

Supplies:
- ❑ Paper, white or colored
- ❑ Tray
- ❑ Scrap paper
- ❑ Ruler
- ❑ Pencils with broken or dull points (or any other tool that is not sharp)
- ❑ Brayers (special rollers used in printmaking)
- ❑ Water-base block print ink
- ❑ Styrofoam sheets or plates
- ❑ Scissors
- ❑ Clean up supplies

When Jesus called the disciples to follow him, he selected men with a variety of qualities. Leadership was probably one of the most important characteristics. Jesus wanted disciples who would be able to lead others and to "be fishers of men."

The symbol most often attributed to Simon is a fish lying on a book. The fish symbolizes his leadership in bringing others to Christ. The book represents the Gospel, the information about Jesus and his teachings. As well as the other disciples, Simon was a leader in the early Christian church. According to tradition, he did mission work in Egypt and Asia Minor. Later he traveled with Jude/Thaddaeus to Persia, where they were both killed.

Make a styrofoam block print of Simon's symbol to remind you to be a leader for Christ. Use the ruler to outline several boxes, about 4" by 5", on the scrap paper. Practice drawing Simon's symbol until it looks the way you like it. Cut a piece of styrofoam 4" x 5" and place it under the symbol you have chosen. Trace over the drawing, pressing hard enough to make an impression in the styrofoam. Remove the paper and retrace the lines with a dull tool. The symbol should be dented in, but do not cut through the foam. Add texture, such as fish scales and details on the book; however, any letters have to be drawn backwards to print properly.

Cover the work area. Squeeze ink from the tube onto a tray or other non-porous surface and spread it out evenly by rolling the brayer back and forth in the ink until it makes a "crackling" sound. Roll the inked roller over the styrofoam block to cover evenly with color. Carefully place blank paper over the inked block; use your thumb to press over the back side of the sheet. Try not to slide the paper. Slowly peel back the print to remove it from the block. Set aside to dry or hang from a clothesline with clips.

When the ink is dry, trim the edges and make note paper by gluing the prints to the front of folded paper. Use the notes to write a "Thank You" to a leader or teacher who has helped you learn more about Jesus. Or, become a "fisher of men" yourself by inviting a friend to worship or church school.

COOPERATION

Supplies:
- ❑ Commercially made potholder weaving kit
- ❑ Hook or shuttle for weaving
- ❑ Instructions
- ❑ Loops, assorted colors
- ❑ Loom

Advance Preparation:
- If instructions for using the loom are not available or are difficult to understand, write them in a simple form for the learning center.

Cooperation was an important quality necessary to be one of Jesus' disciples. Jesus had a short time to teach the twelve men he had chosen; they were intended to carry on his work.

Simon represented a different element of society; it is reported that he was from a radical Jewish sect know as Zealots, who were trying to rid Judea of Roman control. Politically, they were just the opposite of the Publicans which Matthew, the tax collector, represented. They must have had to adjust their thinking to be able to work cooperatively as disciples of Jesus.

Simon's way of life included force and fighting. After becoming one of the disciples, he learned to use his "zeal" for peaceful causes instead of war. Complete this simple weaving activity which illustrates the value of cooperation. Place all of the loops you want in a pile and stretch each one from one side of the loom to the other. Weave the other loops under one and over one, according to the directions for using the loom, until all of the pegs on the loom are covered and fabric is formed. Finish the edges of the potholder as directed by lifting one loop at a time from each peg, chaining one loop inside of the next around the outside of the frame until all are used. Tie a knot at the end to hold the loops in place.

Think about the cooperation involved in the weaving process: the loose loops really do not have much use. The loops stretched on the loom are next to each other, but are not strong enough to be used for anything. However, once the loops are woven together, the potholder becomes a useful piece of sturdy fabric. Take the theme of cooperation one step further and sew together a potholder from everyone in the class to form a large mat or rug.

More can be accomplished when Jesus' disciples, then and now, work together!

INDIVIDUALITY

Supplies:
- ❑ Posterboard
- ❑ Scissors
- ❑ Aluminum foil
- ❑ Glue
- ❑ Construction paper
- ❑ Photograph of each student
- ❑ Markers or crayons
- ❑ Ribbon

One of the unique qualities that Simon the Zealot brought to the job of being one of Jesus' twelve disciples was individuality. When Jesus called him, Simon was a member of a group of fierce fighters that wanted to drive the Roman conquerors out of Israel by force. Jesus molded Simon's quality of "zeal" for driving people away to a quality of "zeal" for bringing people to the Gospel.

Think about the unique qualities that God has given you. Using paper and pencil, list and describe several of these "gifts." These ideas will become part of a personal crest or shield.

Although a shield is a symbol associated with protection and fighting, the shape is also used as a crest to depict personal traits of an individual. Cut a crest shape from posterboard. Cut aluminum foil to fit the crest. Wrap the foil around the shape. Cut a large cross from construction paper and glue it to the center of the crest. If you have a picture of yourself, glue it to the center of the crest. Instead of using an actual photograph, draw a self-portrait and attach it to the shield shape. Draw, color, cut and glue pictures of your interests, abilities and talents to the sections of the crest. Make holes in the top of the crest and tie a ribbon through them to serve as a hanger. Celebrate the gifts that you have been given and the ways in which you use them to serve God.

Chapter Thirteen

Judas Iscariot

Judas Iscariot, the name listed last in the register of the twelve disciples, is generally remembered as the person who betrayed Jesus. Judas was a man whose life was filled with contrasts. Judas was the only disciple from Judea; the others were from Galilee. In his role as one of the first followers, he was entrusted with the position of treasurer, yet in the end he became a traitor. Even his use of the money, at first for good and in the end for evil, was contradictory. Judas' goal, a political kingdom, was in opposition to Jesus' mission, a spiritual kingdom. And, most importantly, Judas' life was characterized by guilt rather than by the forgiveness that the one he betrayed offered to his followers.

Five learning centers explore the life of Judas through the theme of "contrasts." Use the activities to gather information about one of the first twelve disciples and to gain insights about being a follower of Jesus today.

JUDAS ISCARIOT: JUDEAN/GALILEAN

Supplies:
- Pencils
- Glue sticks
- Construction paper, 9" x 12" and 4 1/2" x 6" pieces
- Scrap paper
- Scissors (X-acto knife for older pupils)

Judas Iscariot was the only disciple among the Twelve who was not a Galilean. It is believed that his name means "man of Kerioth," which refers to a town in southern Palestine or Judea. Some historians think that Judas may have been more sophisticated and more shrewd than the rustic and emotional Galileans.[1] Since Judas Iscariot was an "outsider," the other disciples may have misunderstood him and possibly mistrusted him, as well.

Think about some of the contrasts between people who come from other locations: languages may be the same, but spoken with an accent; customs and traditions may be unfamiliar; physical appearance and clothing styles may seem strange. Being different does not mean that one way is right and the other way is wrong...it just means it is DIFFERENT!

Judas and the other disciples probably dealt with lots of opposites while working together. Complete this simple paper collage design and think about contrasts or differences.

Choose two pieces of construction paper, one of each size. Be sure the colors are contrasting—light against dark or bright against dull. Draw a symbol, such as a cross, heart or shield, or a simple outline of a person in the center of the smaller sheet of paper. It may be helpful to try out some designs or shapes on scrap paper first. Carefully, cut out the shape and set aside. Glue the part with the "hole" onto the left half of the 9" x 12" paper. Center the cut-out piece on the right half of the background and glue it in place. Notice that the shape does not change, but the colors are in an opposite position.

JUDAS ISCARIOT: POLITICAL KINGDOM/SPIRITUAL KINGDOM

Supplies:
- Bible
- Pencils
- Protractor
- Scissors
- Paper
- Ruler
- 3" x 5" cards

Very little is known about Judas Iscariot, the last disciple to be chosen by Jesus. Some believe that he was a Zealot, one of the fierce fighters who wanted to bring an end to Roman rule. Judas mistakenly thought that Jesus was going to exert power over Roman leaders and establish an earthly kingdom. He did not understand that Jesus' ministry was about peace and a spiritual kingdom.

Some theories are that Judas was disappointed because Jesus was not the political Messiah or king. Other thoughts include the possibility that Judas may have wanted to betray Jesus to force him to show godly powers by saving himself. Because of his impatience or frustration, Judas took desperate measures and became a traitor.

Construct this special tangram to understand the contrast in goals between Judas and Jesus.

Look up the following passages in the Bible: John 18:36; Matthew 6:33; Mark 10:14,15; Luke 12:32-34; Mark 1:14,15; John 3:3. Read all of the verses and write down on scrap paper the four that you especially like.

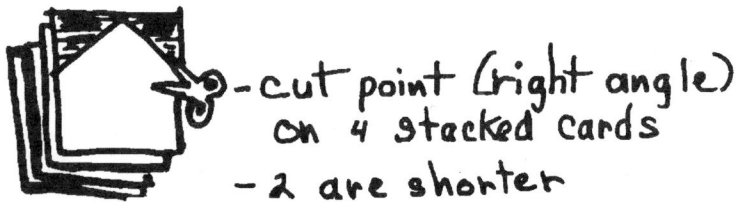
- cut point (right angle) on 4 stacked cards
- 2 are shorter

Take four 3" x 5" note cards — trim one inch from the short end of two cards. Stack the trimmed and untrimmed cards, then cut a point on one end of all four pieces at the same time. A 90° angle will work best.

On just one side of the paper pieces, write the word "Jesus" on all of the points. Turn the pieces over and write the word "Judas" along the edge opposite each point.

Copy the four scripture references you have chosen onto the "Jesus" side of the tangram—one verse per section. If time allows, copy the entire passage. Arrange the "Jesus" pieces with the points touching in the center; be sure to place longer sections with points together and then fit in shorter cards. What shape does this form? This symbol is a reminder of the type of kingdom Jesus talked about.

Now turn the cards over and place the two longest sections side by side, points up, adding one shorter piece to each side. This shape looks like a crown, which signifies the kind of kingdom Judas was hoping for. Can you think of any words to describe how a political kingdom is different from a spiritual one?

JUDAS ISCARIOT: TRUSTED/TRAITOR

Supplies:
- Paper cutter or scissors
- Stapler
- Dictionary
- Markers
- Staples
- Construction paper (cut into 1" strips)

Advance Preparation:
- Write an "everyday" example of betrayal on several of the strips. Prepare one piece for each participant. Examples, which may be repeated, include gossiping, telling secrets, lying, throwing a game and cheating on a test.

After Jesus chose Judas Iscariot as one of the first twelve disciples, he entrusted him with the position of treasurer of the group (John 12:6; 13:29). Since Judas seemed to come from a business background, it was logical that he should handle the finances of the followers. In the end, however, this seemingly loyal leader became a tainted traitor when he delivered Jesus into the hands of his enemies. Judas sold Jesus to the high priests for thirty pieces of silver, about the price of a slave.

Disciples Then! Disciples Now! — 89

Not only did Judas betray the Lord, he also betrayed the trust that had been placed in him. Although this event took place long ago, examples of "betrayal" occur everyday. Telling a secret betrays a confidence; throwing a game betrays a team.

Look in the dictionary for the definition of the word "betrayal." Select a strip of construction paper which has an "everyday" example of betrayal written on it. If desired, choose a blank strip and write a different incident. Think about the situation and the way in which trust was betrayed. What should have been done instead? Pick a contrasting strip of paper and write one idea for changing the situation. For instance, if the first strip reads, "Telling a secret—betrays the trust of another person," the second strip could say, "Since Kim trusted me with her secret, I must not tell it to anyone else." Staple the first strip to form a link, and add the second strip to it to begin a chain. Each person who visits the learning center will continue the process and add his or her loops to the chain. Review each person's ideas.

JUDAS ISCARIOT: MONEY --- GOOD VS. EVIL

Supplies:
- Paper
- Pencils
- Crayons
- Paper clips
- Small boxes or cans with lids
- Tape or glue sticks
- Pattern for shield shape

The name of Judas Iscariot has become a symbol for deception and betrayal. Apparently, Jesus saw qualities in Judas that would be valuable to the group he had selected. Jesus appointed Judas to be the treasurer or accountant for the disciples, which shows that the leader trusted him with an important position.

It is difficult for us to understand why one of Jesus' hand-picked followers would turn against him. Some people think that after Judas joined the Twelve and took charge of the finances, he became greedy. There is a scriptural account of Jesus and Judas disagreeing about the use of money. Read John 12:1-8. Judas asked why expensive perfume was being used for anointing Jesus instead of being sold to help the poor. Jesus gives his explanation to Judas in John 12:7-8. John suspected that Judas' concern was not really for the poor, but for himself.

The Gospel of Matthew reports that Judas was paid thirty pieces of silver to identify Jesus to the high priests so they could arrest him. (Matthew 26:14-16) It is recorded that Judas was sorry for what he had done, tried to stop the authorities, and gave back the money. It seems that Judas' dealings with money matters were contradictory: good versus evil. His business skills and concern for the poor may have been motivated by desire for personal gain. In the end, he was remorseful and could not keep the thirty pieces of silver he had been paid as a bribe.

Because he betrayed Jesus, Judas has not been assigned a traditional symbol. He has been represented by a dingy yellow color for treason or deceit; a piece of rope to show that he died by hanging; coins symbolizing the bribe; and most commonly, a blank shield. Create a crayon etching symbol that includes reminders of Judas Iscariot.

Draw an outline of a shield or trace one using a pattern. Color heavily with a yellow crayon, cut out the blank shield and set aside. Draw or trace the second shield, color heavily with yellow or white crayon, then cover the light color with black crayon.

Bend open one end of a paper clip to use as an etching tool. Scratch into the black surface to create symbols of coins and rope. As you scrape away the black crayon, the underneath color will show through. Cut out the etched shield.

Tape or glue the two shields to a bank you have or make a bank by cutting a slit into the lid of a small container. As you save coins, think about ways to use the money for a good cause.

JUDAS ISCARIOT: GUILT/FORGIVENESS

Supplies:

- Bible(s)
- One or two beanbags
- Masking tape
- Bible dictionary or concordance
- Index cards (20)
- Marker

Advance Preparation:

- Prepare two sets of index cards, numbered from 1-10. Tape one set, in a tile pattern, to the learning center table or to the floor. On the second set, write a scripture verse related to forgiveness on each card. Refer to a Bible dictionary or concordance for verses to use. Include both Old and New Testament examples.

Although there are many contrasts in the life of Judas Iscariot, perhaps the greatest is guilt vs. forgiveness. After Judas arranged to lead the Lord into the hands of his enemies, he was overcome with guilt. Judas returned to the high priests with the money they had given him. He wanted to call off the deal. They would not hear of it, nor would they take back the money. Judas threw down the thirty pieces of silver, saying, "I have sinned in that I have betrayed innocent blood." Then he went out and took his own life. It is reported that the authorities used the money to buy a burial ground, commonly referred to as the "Field of Blood."

Contrast this situation to the fact that Jesus, the person Judas betrayed, died on the cross to offer forgiveness to all who believe in him. Instead of being overcome with guilt, Judas could have experienced God's abundant love—if he had only repented and asked for forgiveness. Look up II Corinthians 5:19. Paul writes that "in Christ God was reconciling the world to himself, not counting their trespasses against them." Judas was included in this act of reconciliation, however it seems that he chose not to believe or accept it.

Disciples Then! Disciples Now!

The Bible is filled with stories of people who sinned and were forgiven. Play a game of "Bean Bag Toss" to help remember several of these accounts. Toss a beanbag into one of the numbered squares. Select the card with the same number as the square. Look up the scripture passage and read the story of forgiveness. Continue playing as time and interest allow.

[1]Brownrigg, Ronald. *The Twelve Apostles*. New York: Mackmillan, 1974.

Chapter Fourteen

Matthias

After Jesus' ascension, the eleven remaining disciples decided to choose a replacement for Judas Iscariot. The man selected to complete the number twelve needed to be someone who had been with Jesus throughout his entire ministry. He also needed to be a person who had been an eyewitness to the Lord's resurrection. Matthias, a faithful follower, was elected. Learn more about Matthias by using the activities in these five learning centers. Review the significance of the number twelve, remember the criteria for selecting the replacement, re-emphasize the importance of prayer, research a historical symbol and represent discipleship today in a concrete way. A teaching tool or technique associated with the theme of "rocks" connects the five topics.

MATTHIAS: REASON FOR REPLACEMENT

Supplies:
- List of the original twelve disciples
- Chalk, masking tape or carpet squares
- Rocks

One of the reasons the eleven disciples felt the responsibility of replacing Judas Iscariot was because of the importance attached to the number twelve. Jesus had made it clear to the disciples that just as there had been twelve tribes of Israel through whom God would bless all the nations of the earth, twelve apostles were to be instruments through whom God would proclaim the good news to all the world. Jesus had entrusted to the Twelve this great mission (John 14:25-27; Matthew 10:1-42). He had promised the Twelve that in his kingdom they would sit on twelve thrones, judging the twelve tribes of Israel (Matthew 19:18; Luke 22:30). It is no wonder that the first item on the agenda after the Lord's ascension was to find a replacement for Judas Iscariot and to keep the movement intact.

Review the names of the original twelve disciples and report information about their lives and work. Draw a hopscotch game, including twelve spaces, in chalk on cement or mark it with masking tape or carpet squares on a floor. Number the squares one through twelve. Write information about the disciples in each of the squares, or on corresponding slips of paper. For example:

1. Rock [Peter]
2. Tax Collector [Matthew]

3. Nathanael [Bartholomew]
4. Traitor [Judas]
5. The Less [James]
6. Beloved [John]
7. Doubter [Thomas]
8. The Zealot [Simon]
9. Thaddaeus [Jude]
10. Questioner [Philip]
11. Five Thousand [Andrew]
12. Son of Zebedee [James]

Play the game by throwing a rock into one of the numbered squares. Read the word or phrase written in the square and name the disciple described. Remember to hop to the end of the game and back, being careful to hop on one foot in the single squares, land on both feet in the double squares and hop over the square that holds the rock.

MATTHIAS: CRITERIA FOR SELECTION

Supplies:
- ❑ Drawing paper
- ❑ Markers or colored chalk
- ❑ Scissors
- ❑ Gray construction paper
- ❑ Brass paper fasteners
- ❑ Bible atlas or Bible handbook

As the disciples gathered to choose a replacement for Judas Iscariot, Peter stated that the person selected should have been one of Jesus' followers from the time of his baptism. The necessary criteria for the new disciple were his witness of the resurrection of Jesus and his divine selection.

Matthias and Joseph, called Barsabbas or Justus, were considered qualified. The group prayed for guidance from the Holy Spirit before "casting lots," or voting by throwing stones with the names written on them. Matthias was elected to become the new disciple.

In this activity, create a picture with a symbol of Jesus' resurrection—the stone rolled away from the tomb. This will serve as a reminder of the important gauge for choosing Judas' substitute, and of the standard for being Jesus' followers today: being a witness of the resurrection.

Study pictures in Bible reference books to learn what type of tomb was used for burial in Jesus' time. Choose a piece of paper and draw the cave, plants, trees and people.

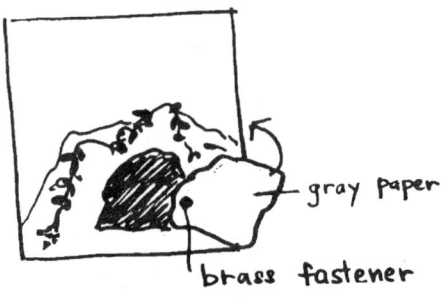

Tear or cut a rock shape from the gray paper, making certain the piece is large enough to cover the cave opening. Use a scissor point to punch a small hole in the "rock" and into the picture, near the bottom of the tomb. Poke the fastener through the rock and attach it to the picture.

"Roll the stone away" by moving the gray paper piece away from the tomb opening. Remember what the resurrection means to us as modern day disciples.

94 — *Disciples Then! Disciples Now!*

MATTHIAS: PRAYER FOR GUIDANCE

Supplies:

- ❑ Felt squares, bright colors
- ❑ Light colored chalk
- ❑ Thread, assorted colors
- ❑ Pinking shears (optional)
- ❑ Sharp scissors
- ❑ Heart patterns
- ❑ Needle
- ❑ Bible

Before casting lots to choose the replacement for Judas Iscariot, Peter led the voters in prayer. In Acts 1:24-25, Peter prayed, "Lord, you know every heart. Show us which one of these two you have chosen to take the place in this ministry and apostleship from which Judas turned aside to go to his own place."

This prayer is important because it was a simple request for wisdom and guidance. It was the first recorded prayer spoken by the disciples, as a group, after the resurrection. The disciples understood that God has the power to change any situation.

When the lots were cast, Matthias was chosen ... an answer to prayer. It is interesting to note that his name means "gift of Jehovah."

Sew a felt mola as a reminder that God knows every heart. A mola is a South American form of reverse applique. Instead of sewing designs on the surface, layers of fabric are sewn together and the design is cut away to reveal underneath colors. Use a heart symbol for the design.

If felt squares are 9" x 12", cut them in half. Choose two or three contrasting colors of felt. Stack the rectangles and sew them together, about 3/4 inch in from the edge. Carefully trim so all of the edges are even; pinking shears give an attractive finish.

Place the mola vertically or horizontally in front of you and trace a heart pattern onto the top piece of felt. Chalk or a dressmaker's pencil will show up on the felt. Choose a contrasting or matching color of thread and sew along the heart outline. Use a small running stitch to sew through all of the felt layers. Very carefully cut through just the top layer of felt, following along the inside edge of the heart outline. Lift out the heart, exposing the color underneath.

Older learners might enjoy cutting a smaller heart to expose a third layer of felt. Keep the finished heart mola as a prayer prompter to remind you that God knows what is in your heart. Read Ezekiel 11:19,20 and Ezekiel 36:26 and remember that God wants his followers to have a heart filled with love rather than a heart of stone.

MATTHIAS: HISTORICAL SYMBOL

Supplies:
- Ceiling tile or 8" x 8" wood or heavy cardboard
- Pea gravel or aquarium gravel (available in many colors)
- Tacky glue or craft cement
- Paper
- Glue brushes
- Trays or shallow cake pans
- Pencils
- Carbon paper
- Pictures of ax and Bible
- Small margarine cups with lids for gravel

Very little is known about Matthias after he was chosen to be a disciple. It is believed that he wrote a book called The Traditions Of Matthias. The book is lost, but several historians have quoted his sayings. Some writers report that he was stoned to death and others say he was beheaded for preaching the Gospel. Traditionally, the symbol for Matthias is an ax and an open Bible.

Assemble a stone mosaic depicting the shield of Matthias. Remember that many of the disciples are assigned a symbol that relates to the way they died. Most of the group died as they went about sharing the teachings of Jesus. Would you be brave enough to be a disciple?

Study the pictures of an ax and an open Bible. Create your own symbol for Matthias or trace one that is provided. Use simple outline shapes for your mosaic design. Transfer the design onto the square base with carbon paper. Brush or dab glue onto a small section of the symbol and begin to fill in with the colored gravel. You may have to experiment to determine how much glue will be needed. Continue working in small areas until the entire symbol is covered. You may wish to fill in the background with pea gravel or aquarium gravel of a contrasting color.

For a successful mosaic, be certain that the shapes and outlines are distinct and carefully glued. After a few days, add glue if the stones are loose. Add a frame or special picture hanging supplies if you wish to display the finished product.

Review the shields of the other disciples. How many can you identify? What would your personal symbol include?

96 — Disciples Then! Disciples Now!

YOU: COMMITMENT TO DISCIPLESHIP

Supplies:

- Large rocks
- Permanent markers or paint and brushes

One of the requirements for the newly elected disciple, Matthias, was that he was a witness to the resurrection of Jesus. As modern day disciples, we too are called to be witnesses of God's love. Jesus' mission and ministry continues today.

Choose a large rock that can be used as a doorstop—a method of keeping the door open as a reminder to spread God's love by telling others about the life, death and resurrection of Jesus. Paint or color the rock with symbols representing ways to be a modern day disciple. Words such as home and school, and pictures like a Bible and praying hands are appropriate. Place the rock in a place where it will be a visual symbol of commitment to Christ.

Chapter Fifteen

Conclusion

Conclude the study of Jesus' special followers by using a series of learning centers that review and reinforce the theme "Disciples Then! Disciples Now!" Five activities, each involving the number twelve, are provided. "Symbols of Service" reviews the emblems and crests associated with the disciples; "Names to Know" offers a game with a hidden message; "Riddles for Review" re-examines information about the chosen followers; "Scenes of Stories" relates to twelve New Testament scripture passages associated with Jesus and the disciples; and "Disciples Day by Day" reminds participants that following Jesus is a 365 days a year opportunity. Use the five activities to put the theme of discipleship into a biblical, historical and modern day perspective.

SYMBOLS OF SERVICE

Supplies:
- Embroidery hoops (or other type of eight inch or ten inch ring)
- Small shield patterns, approximately two inches by three inches
- Bible dictionaries or other reference materials
- Ribbon, 1-2 inches wide
- Note cards, unlined
- Pencils
- Scissors
- Fine-tipped markers
- Tape
- Picture of traditional fish symbol
- String
- Glue
- Ball point pens

There were many men and women who followed Jesus as he traveled throughout the Jordan Valley and around the Sea of Galilee. Jesus carefully selected twelve men to help with his teaching and ministry. As there were twelve tribes of Israel, Jesus purposely called twelve special followers to represent the "New Israel." Each one of the men had something important to contribute to the ministry of Jesus. And, in addition, the specially chosen disciples, sometimes designated as "the Twelve," were commissioned to carry on the ministry of Jesus after he was no longer on the earth.

Traditionally, each disciple was assigned an emblem which highlighted his personal characteristics or illustrated the way he died. In Christian art, the symbols have been portrayed most often within the form of a shield. Refer to the following list, then determine which symbols to use for a ribbon banner project featuring the emblems attributed to each of the Twelve. Read the previous chapters of <u>Disciples Then! Disciples Now!</u> for descriptions of each disciple's design, or check reference materials for the most commonly used symbols.

SYMBOLS FOR DISCIPLES

Peter
Fish; Cock; Rock; Keys; Inverted Latin cross
Andrew
X-shaped cross on blue background
James the Great (son of Zebedee)
Three scallop shells
John
Serpent and chalice; Cauldron with oil; Eagle
Philip
Loaves of bread, some depict 2, others show 5; Cross
Bartholomew
One knife or three knives in a row
Thomas
Carpenter's square and a spear
Matthew
Three money pouches
James The Less (son of Alphaeus)
Saw or club
Jude/Thaddaeus
Sailing ship
Simon The Zealot
Fish lying on top of a book
Judas Iscariot
Rope and pouch with thirty pieces of silver; Yellow, blank shield
Matthias
Ax and open Bible

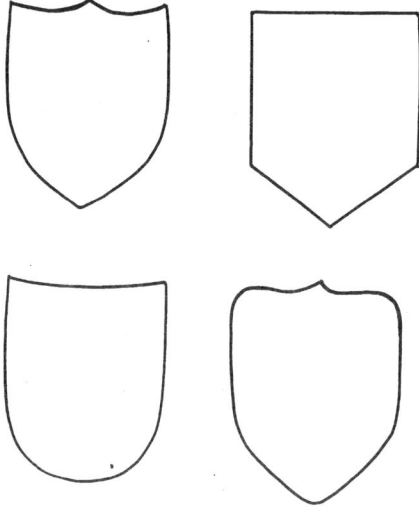

Begin constructing the "Symbols Banner" by cutting thirteen pieces of ribbon to lengths varying between 10" to 15". Set them aside.

Draw or trace shields and symbols for each of the disciples. Add color and details with markers, then cut out the shapes. With small tape circles or a little bit of glue, attach each shield to a different piece of ribbon. Vary the placement of the symbols to prevent having all of the shapes at the bottom of the ribbons.

Press firmly with a ball point pen to print the name of each disciple on the ribbon bearing his shield. Fasten the ribbons to the ring with small pieces of tape; if using a hoop, tighten the outside ring firmly around the inner ring. Tie strings to the circle in three places to help balance the ribbon banner, then tie the strings together at the top to allow for hanging.

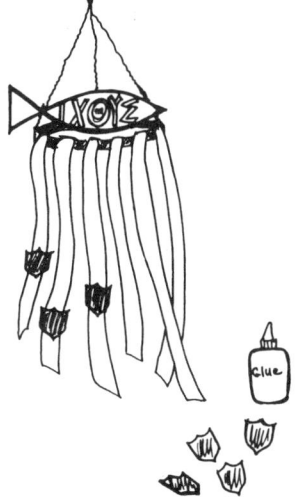

Complete the "Ribbon Banner" by adding another symbol to it. There were many other "disciples" of Jesus in addition to the chosen twelve. In early Christian times people were punished for following the teachings of Jesus, so they held their meetings in private. Christians used a simple fish shape as a secret symbol to let other believers know who they were and where they were meeting. The letters in the Greek word fish, Ichthus, are the first letters in the word Jesus Christ, God's son, savior. The fish is still a symbol for Christian disciples today. Add a fish emblem to the ribbon banner. Trace or draw the fish symbol and attach it to the strings. In the center of the fish, print the Greek letters IXOYC or the word Jesus. Hang the banner for all to see!

NAMES TO KNOW

Supplies:
- ❑ Bible
- ❑ Paper
- ❑ Game sheets
- ❑ Pencils

Advance Preparation:
- Duplicate one copy of the game sheet for each participant.

What do you remember about Jesus' disciples? Can you name the twelve men especially chosen by him? Can you recall something unique about each disciple? Solve this word puzzle as a way to review what you have learned about the distinctive group of men called to carry on the teaching and ministry of Jesus.

Consider the clues given to identify the disciples.

Check your answers by finding the list of disciples in your Bible. Look in Matthew 10:2-4, Mark 3:16-19 or Luke 6:14-16. Read all of the references mentioned, plus information about the replacement for Judas Iscariot. (Acts 1:15-26)

Fill in the blanks and pay special attention to the letters that are emphasized. When all of the names are listed, arrange the emphasized letters to discover the surprise answer to this question: WHAT IS A BAKER'S DOZEN? When you have completed the puzzle, explain how the mystery words apply to this special group of men chosen to continue the teaching and ministry of Jesus.

PUZZLE

Replacement for Judas Iscariot _ _ _ _ _ _ _ _

Betrayed Jesus _ _ _ _ _ _ _ _ _ _ _ _ _

Doubted Jesus' Resurrection _ _ _ _ _ _

Cananaean _ _ _ _ _ _ _ _ _ _ _ _ _ _

A son of Alphaeus _ _ _ _ _ _ _ _ _ _ _ _

Peter's brother _ _ _ _ _ _

First chosen; other name Simon _ _ _ _ _

Helped to feed the 5000 _ _ _ _ _ _

Last name, Lebbaeus _ _ _ _ _ _ _ _ _

A son of Zebedee _ _ _ _ _ _ _ _ _ _ _ _ _

Also called Nathanael _ _ _ _ _ _ _ _ _ _ _

One of the sons of Thunder _ _ _ _

Tax collector _ _ _ _ _ _ _

ANSWERS

```
           MATTHIAS
        JUDASISCARIOT
           THOMAS
       SIMONTHEZEALOT
         JAMESTHELESS
            ANDREW
            PETER
            PHILIP
          THADDAEUS
         JAMESTHEGREAT
         BARTHOLOMEW
             JOHN
            MATTHEW
```

A BAKER'S DOZEN = A DOZEN PLUS ONE

RIDDLES FOR REVIEW

Supplies:
- ❏ Bible
- ❏ Paper
- ❏ Riddle game
- ❏ Pencils or pens

Riddles are word puzzles that are fun to figure out and also fun to write. Review information about Jesus' twelve disciples by answering the riddles on the game sheet. Each disciple's name is used once. Read each riddle and write the name of the correct person in the blank.

After completing the game, try writing more riddles. Leave them in the learning center and challenge other participants to answer them.

Riddles:

1. Beloved disciple is what Jesus called me;
I was a part of the inner circle of three.
Who am I? _____

2. My brother and I left our fishing behind;
I brought others to Jesus, the Savior to find.
Who am I? _____

3. My Lord and my God were the words that I said
When I believed that Jesus arose from the dead.
Who am I? _____

4. Some people think bad thoughts when they hear my name.
I betrayed the Savior and that is my shame.
Who am I? _____

5. I always had questions and yet I still knew
Jesus was the Messiah; that's very true.
Who am I? _____

6. Even a tax collector was chosen to serve.
I wrote down the stories, God's love to preserve.
Who am I? _____

7. People connect lots of numbers with me—
One number is one and another is three.
Who am I? _____

8. Although I was chosen at the very end,
I always served Jesus and loved him as friend.
Who am I? _____

9. One of my symbol's is the scallop shell.
In the country of Spain they remember me well.
Who am I? _____

Disciples Then! Disciples Now! — 103

10. Thaddaeus and Lebbaeus are two of my names,
But a heart of compassion is my claim to fame.
Who am I? _____

11. Strong willed is what they called the fighter in me.
I wanted a kingdom that others could see.
Who am I? _____

12. One name starts with N, and the other with a B;
Together they are part of my family history.
Who am I? _____

13. Alphaeus is connected with me.
Others had my first name, you see.
Who am I? _____

Answers

1. John
2. Andrew
3. Thomas
4. Judas Iscariot
5. Philip
6. Matthew
7. Simon Peter
8. Matthias
9. James the Greater
10. Jude/Thaddaeus
11. Simon The Zealot
12. Bartholomew/Nathanael
13. James The Less

SCENES OF STORIES

Supplies:
- Bible
- Pencils
- Paper for making notes
- Paints
- Paintbrushes
- Markers
- Clean-up supplies
- Masking tape
- Paper rolls in a variety of sizes for mini, midi or maxi murals

There are many wonderful stories in the Bible! Some of the most vivid pictures or most "colorful" accounts of Jesus and his disciples appear in the Gospels, Matthew, Mark, Luke and John, and in the book of Acts. You may find favorite disciple stories in many other sections of the New Testament. Here is a list of twelve scripture references for you to read. Try to visualize what the setting would look like and what activities are taking place.

Matthew 4:18-22 — Calls first disciples
Matthew 8:23-27 — Jesus calms the storm

Matthew 14:13-21 — Feeding the 5000
Mark 6:45-52 — Jesus walks on water
Mark 9:2-13 — Jesus' transfiguration
Mark 10:13-16 — Jesus blesses little children
Luke 19:28-40 — Triumphal entry into Jerusalem
Luke 22:7-13 — Passover dinner in the Upper Room
John 13:1-5 — Jesus washes disciples' feet
John 13:21-30 — Jesus foretells his betrayal
Acts 1:6-11 — The ascension of Jesus
Acts 2:1-13 —The coming of the Holy Spirit

Now that your "mind's eye" is filled with colorful action pictures, it is time to create a mural or part of a mural for a visual record of what you have learned. After choosing the event or story you wish to illustrate, select the paper size best for your mural. Adding machine tape works well for a mini mural. Use fine-tipped markers or tiny brushes for details. A medium-sized painting can be done on a roll of shelf paper or plain newsprint. If there are other artists available to help, create a life-size mural by tracing each other in various positions on large paper. After the large scenes and figures are painted, join the sections with tape for a maxi mural!

Display the masterpieces for all to see. Be prepared to explain what is happening in the mural...tell the story!

DISCIPLES DAY BY DAY

Supplies:
- Photographs and pictures from many sources
- Calendar pages for each month, blank
- Paper, 11" x 17", seven sheets per calendar
- Stapler
- Staples
- Scissors
- Glue
- Markers

Being one of Jesus' disciples is a 365 days a year commitment! Make and use calendars that illustrate ways to be a disciple today. Different pictures will be used each month to illustrate ways to be a disciple at home, school, church and numerous other places. Begin by brainstorming one way to be a disciple each month. Choose a blank piece of paper and write the names of the months down the left side of it. On the right side of the page jot down one or more ways to show that you are Jesus' disciple. For example:

- January — Shovel a homebound person's sidewalk (if you live in a snowy place) or do yard work for a shut-in;
- February — Send a Valentine to someone who might not be remembered;
- March — Fly a kite proclaiming God's love;
- April — Read a book about a person of faith;
- May — Invite someone new in the neighborhood to play a game;
- June — Ask a friend to a special program at church, such as Vacation Bible School;
- July — Become involved in a special project to take care of God's creation;
- August — Take care of a younger child or groom a pet;
- September — Eat lunch with someone you don't know very well;
- October — Learn a new way to use your gifts and skills;
- November — Give a thankful offering to a special cause;
- December — Give a gift of time or talent.

To make your calendar, choose seven pieces of paper. The paper can be any size, however, a large size such as 11" x 17" allows more room to create interesting, inviting pictures. Fold the seven pages in half and staple the sheets in the middle, on the crease line. Create each month's illustration of "discipleship" from a different method involving photographs and pictures. Twelve suggestions include using pictures from magazines, cards, snapshots, school newspapers, local and national newspapers, postcards, brochures, newspaper inserts, stickers, other calendars, catalogs and posters. Using basic tools such as markers, scissors and glue, use the twelve top sections of the calendar to create different illustrations of ways to be a disciple today. To make the pages for each month, dates may be copied off of another calendar, or calendar pages may be duplicated and glued to the bottom of each respective sheet. Design a cover and write additional information about discipleship on the remaining blank pages. Write your name somewhere on the calendar.

Hang the completed calendar in a special place in the classroom or at home. Remember to be a disciple every day.

Simon Peter

James the Less
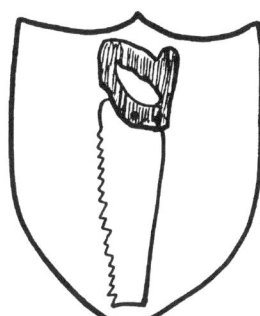

Thomas

Andrew
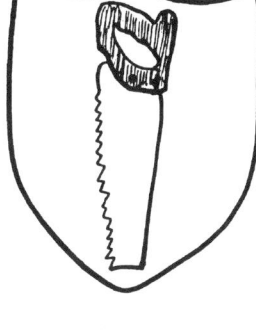

Bartholomew
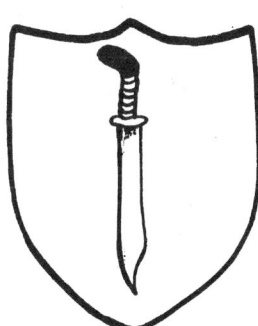

Philip

Simon the Zealot

James the Greater

Judas Iscariot
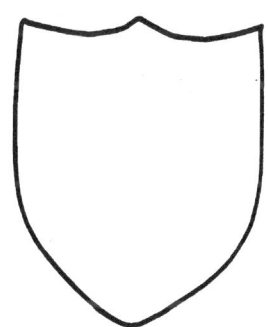

John

Matthew

Judas (Thaddeus)

Matthias

Disciples Then! Disciples Now! — 107

Chapter Sixteen

Adaptations

Although the information and ideas contained in the book <u>Disciples Then! Disciples Now!</u> are presented in a learning center format, the contents and concepts can be easily adapted for use in various worship, education, outreach and nurture settings within a congregation. Try the suggestions for "twelve" areas of ministry and add others to modify the material and methods to meet specific situations and circumstances.

Adult Bible Study
- Research and report on the customs and culture of the time in which the disciples lived.
- Study a "Disciple of the Month"—Biblical, historical and/or modern day.

Children's Church/Worship
- Create a children's bulletin using many of the "paper and pencil" activities from the learning centers.
- Incorporate the symbol for each disciple into a series of object lessons.

Confirmation Classes
- Interview members of the congregation, such as pastors, church school teachers and youth group leaders who have demonstrated discipleship by words and actions.
- Prepare first person monologues on the lives of the disciples, including specific characteristics needed for modern day followers.

Intergenerational Events
- Depict the life of each disciple in a "Living Tableau," a representation of a scene by an individual or a group dressed in costume.
- Highlight information about the disciples in a "This is Your Life" format.

Outreach
- Become involved in a local, regional, national or international project that demonstrates discipleship.
- Hold a "Missions Festival" featuring countries associated with the outreach of the disciples.

Retreats
- Match each of the original disciples with a historical or modern day person and use the information as the basis of a retreat for families, age groups or classes.
- Show videos on a discipleship theme.

Church School
- Make a mural or bulletin board picturing the life of each disciple.
- Present a program, such as a puppet show, illustrating each disciple's relationship to Jesus.

Vacation Bible School
- Design a Vacation Bible School program on the theme of discipleship.
- Integrate the learning center activities into a Bible times setting.

Week Day Programs ---- After School Care; Kid's Clubs
- Organize an art exhibit of items created in the learning centers.
- Teach hymns and hymn stories on discipleship themes.

Women's & Men's Groups
- Adopt a child in the church as a prayer partner or begin a mentorship program between adults and young people.
- Base an adult/child event, such as a Mother/Daughter or Father/son banquet, on the lives of the disciples.

Worship
- Display banners containing the symbols of the disciples.
- Preach a sermon series on the lives of the disciples or the theme of discipleship.

Youth Groups

- Initiate a service project, short-term or long-term, to demonstrate the theme of following Jesus.
- Produce a video on discipleship in action.

Educator's Meditation

The Story Of The Twelve

"Stop everything and come with me!" Chris exclaimed as she burst through the door of the Parish Resource Center on a cold, icy day in February. "Merrill Pharmacy just put their card racks outside," she continued. "They're giving them away free. Stop everything! Let's go! We need this equipment at the Center. Whatever else you're doing can wait! Come on!"

Shocked by her interruption and stunned by her insistence, I left everything, put on my coat, got in her car and went to the drug store. Panting, we ran through the door, found an employee, and asked for the shelves. The racks would be given, we were informed, to the first people who physically took them from the front of the store. Quickly we asked to use the phone, but were told that it was out of order. Going outside, we slid on the icy sidewalk to the restaurant on the corner, only to discover that it had closed early due to the bad weather. Spotting a telephone outside, we hurried to it, but found that the money stuck in the coin slot prevented the phone from working, and us from making a call. Walking across the street to the 7-11 store, we discovered that the phone in the booth was missing the receiver. Continuing down the block we came to a used car dealership. After telling our story the employee offered to let us make a call. And, after all that, Chris finally reached her husband at work only to learn that his employee who owned a truck was off sick!

Keeping one eye on the pharmacy across the street, the pressure to produce a truck became more intense as we watched the increasing number of people stopping and spotting the shelves! Deciding that our only course of action was to rent the large U-Haul truck in front of the used car company, I completed the paperwork while Chris darted across the street to stand guard over the shelves. Never having driven a truck of that size before, I cautiously maneuvered the machine out of the drive-way, around the block, and to the front of the drug store. With those obstacles behind us, the next challenge was lifting the shelving units onto the back of the U-Haul. Realizing the impossibility of the situation, and still consumed with the desire for the equipment, we went into the store and pleaded for help from the men constructing the new display racks. Possibly assuming that the only way to get rid of us was to offer their assistance, the crew lifted the heavy units onto the truck.

Although the drive to the Center was less than a mile, it seemed like an endless journey. Arriving at our destination, we had more obstacles to overcome. First, there was no one to unload the truck, and second, there was no lock on the back to prevent someone else from taking our treasure. After backing the vehicle into the bushes to make theft less tempting, we started the search for strong bodies who could easily be bribed with pizza in exchange for work. Within the next few hours, the truck was unloaded, the shelves were put into place, the resources were moved to their new location, and the U-Haul was safely returned. The end of the story ... or, the beginning of another.

Throughout the entire adventure a familiar Bible story kept coming to mind. It had striking similarities to the shelf situation. It was the story of Jesus' call to his twelve disciples ... those familiar passages recorded in Matthew, Mark, Luke and John. "Stop. Leave everything. Come with me." Jesus called twelve men from their daily occupations, among them Simon and Andrew from casting a net into the lake, James and John from mending their fishing equipment and Matthew from writing in his tax ledger. I've often wondered how the twelve felt. Startled, stunned, surprised, shocked, scared? For a few minutes, with Chris' interruption in my life and her insistence on my leaving, I caught a glimpse of some of their emotions. "Stop. Leave everything and follow me. Anything else that you are doing is not as important as what I am asking you to do now." Challenge. Commitment. Call.

Being called to move shelves stimulated a new awareness of the call which we, as Christ's followers, have received to be Jesus' disciples today. It almost made the subject of discipleship real, recognizable and relevant. Ordinary people doing extraordinary things because they allow God to work in their lives. Through this humorous, humbling, human experience, I was vividly reminded that I was called to follow Jesus in a unique way. I was called to equip others—to literally fill empty shelves with resources that would strengthen and support the ministries of many people.

Just as the first twelve disciples spread the message of Jesus to people throughout the world, we each need to look at what we can do to spread the message of Christ today—in our own situations and circumstances. How can we use our gifts of call and mission to show that we are one of Jesus' followers? Look at your own life. When and how have you been called? Perhaps you've answered the call to teach a church school class, lead a youth group or start a new Children's ministry. Perhaps God is calling you to follow in a new way—to work in an administrative rather than a teaching role; to become involved in a neighborhood or community ministry; to begin a program to meet the needs of a special group of people.

The story continues, because every time I look at the shelves, I recognize myself in the call of the twelve disciples, and realize how God works in my life. Every time I look at the shelves, I remember that, just like the first twelve disciples, I am called to learn, to listen, to love and to lead, too. Every time I look at those shelves...By the way, did I mention that there were twelve of them?

Resources

Attwater, Donald. The Penguin Dictionary of Saints. Harmondsworth, Middlesex, England: Penguin Books, 1965.

Banter, Nicola. Children's Atlas of the Bible. New York: Smithmark Publishers, 1992.

Bentley, James. A Calendar of Saints. London: Orbis, 1986.

Brownrigg, Ronald. The Twelve Apostles. New York: Macmillan, 1974.

Calvacoressi, Peter. Who's Who in the Bible. New York: Viking, 1987.

Davis, Michael. Young Reader's Book of Christian Symbolism. Nashville, TN: Abingdon, 1967.

Editors. Great People of the Bible and How They Lived. Pleasantville, NY: Reader's Digest, 1974.

Editors. Jesus and the Twelve. Gastonia, NC: Good Will Publishers, 1969.

Editors. Saints and Feast Days. Lives of the Saints: With a Calendar and Ways to Celebrate. Chicago: Loyola University Press, 1985.

Huxhold, Harry N. Twelve Who Followed. Minneapolis: Augsburg, 1987.

Keeley, Robin, Editor. The Message of the Bible. San Diego, CA: Lion Publishing for Guideposts, 1988.

Luedtke, Ralph, Editor. Ideals: Easter. Milwaukee, WI: Ideals, 1977.

Luedtke, Ralph, Editor. Ideals: Easter. Milwaukee, WI: Ideals, 1980.

Oursler, Fulton and April Oursler Armstrong. The Greatest Faith Ever Known. Garden City, NY: Doubleday, 1953.

Rusk, Rev. John. The Story of Christ and His Apostles. N.P.: L.H. Walter, 1912.

Ryan, Lynda. Disciples Biographies: Booklet & Church Bulletin Inserts. San Antonio, TX: Christian Drama Ministries, 1991.

Sanders, E. P. People from the Bible: New Testament. Wilton, CN: Morehouse-Barlow, 1989.

Senterfitt, Marilyn. Celebrate Jesus. Carthage, IL: Shining Star, 1988.

Thompson, J. A. Handbook of Life in Bible Times. Downers Grove, IL: Inter-Varsity Press for Guideposts, 1986.

Vann, Father Joseph, O.F.M., Editor. Lives of Saints With Excerpts from Their Writings. New York: John J. Crawley, 1954.

Woodrow, Martin. People from the Bible: Old Testament. Wilton, CN: Morehouse-Barlow, 1989.